MW01284592

VOICES FROM THE
GRAVEYARD

Early Settlers of Winchester, Indiana

SHARON E. SMITH

Geoff,

Enjoy the history

Sharon E. Smith

Copyright © 2013 Sharon E. Smith
All Rights Reserved.

ISBN-10: 1484903692
ISBN-13: 9781484903698

Library of Congress Control Number: 2013909093
CreateSpace Independent Publishing Platform
North Charleston, South Carolina

The Old Winchester Graveyard

What draws me to this place, where everyone is dead?

Gravestones are gone, or broken or worn, unable to be read.

Generations have gone by since they breathed their last,

Yet I feel so very close to these people of our past.

Once they, like us, walked with strength in their step,

Lives full of dreams, purposes and goals to be met.

Fate and hope brought them here, pioneers on the plains,

Clearing, planting and building to secure all their gains.

Their struggles were many, their diseases without cure,

But their determination to succeed assured us a future.

I come here with respect, love and honor I give,

To those who came first to this place where I live.

I come here to reflect, because it is peaceful and still,

On the value of all lives, and the memories they fill.

So while this old graveyard may be a part of our past,

This great treasure of history, I want it to last.

February, 2005
Sharon E. Smith

Dedication

This book is dedicated to Joseph Casey, a teacher, who taught me that I can write; to my two sons, Eric and Brent Wiltshire, who taught me how to be immensely proud; and to my husband, Robert R. Smith, who taught me that you can fall in love at any age, and that you can come home.

TABLE OF CONTENTS

INTRODUCTION

The first white settlers arrived in what would become Winchester, Indiana in 1816, the same year that Indiana achieved statehood. Two years later Randolph County was incorporated with the town of Winchester its seat. These first settlers faced harsh conditions, severe winters, hot summers and diseases without cure. The land was unending forest inhabited by Indians. These settlers, our predecessors and ancestors, left us a legacy. They left cleared land to sow, a city with houses and businesses, a plan for how to live together and a value system. For this we owe them our thanks and our respect.

After their deaths they were usually buried in one of three cemeteries. The first one, Conway Cemetery, was located where the South East St. parking lot for the Nazarene Church is now. That site was found to be unsuitable and the remains of those buried there were moved. In 1844 the Heaston Cemetery was established and was used until the 1890's. In 1880, land for the Fountain Park Cemetery was donated to the city by Ashal Stone. Some of the remains of those buried in the Heaston Cemetery were moved to Fountain Park, but most were not moved.

This book is about those pioneers, settlers and soldiers whose remains are still in the old Heaston cemetery, now called by most in the community the "Old Winchester Graveyard." It is located in the southwest part of Winchester, on Western Avenue, next to the National Guard Armory.

Unfortunately, records of burials in the Old Winchester were never kept. There is a plat that provides the placement of grave sites, but no record of who is buried where. With so little information, how could the community resurrect this historic site, the final resting place for most of our earliest settlers? A better question is how could the community allow this site to become a memory when the people buried there provided our legacy?

A group of community members began working together in 2004 to restore this site. Everyone on the committee knew that we would never be able to provide the names of everyone buried there. But we knew that we could restore and replace memorial markers that were strewn about the graveyard, mostly under the soil. We knew that we could identify many of our first settlers. We knew we could provide the community a place to visit and study the history of Winchester through its first citizens. And most importantly, we knew that we could honor the memory of these first settlers by restoring their graveyard and by treating the site respectfully.

Research and work began immediately. Through the efforts and donations of many sincere and hard working people, the restoration of the cemetery is now complete. We know the names of 276 persons buried there. We have found and restored 157 complete or partial gravestones. The history of those buried there is an important element of our heritage. The grave markers themselves tell us a lot about our past and the customs of the time. Together they represent a priceless historical record.

This book was created to help "bring to life" the people who are buried in the Old Winchester Graveyard. By reading this you will learn about the lives of these pioneers and how they contributed to the history of the Winchester community.

For a comprehensive historical perspective of Winchester and Randolph County from its earliest period I recommend <u>The History of Randolph County</u>, 1882, written by Ebeneazer Tucker. In my opinion it is a history book without equal. The book is available at the Randolph County Historical Society Museum, 416 S. Meridian Street, Winchester, Indiana 47394.

No project of this magnitude could be accomplished without the combined efforts of many people. Special thanks to the members of the committee who believed and cared, to the local people, service clubs and charitable foundations who donated money to make the project possible, to the talented and dedicated restorationists who brought the graveyard back to life and most importantly to those whose memories we honor for giving us our legacy.

The Restoration Committee*

Bobby and Beverly Manning
Steve Croyle
Monisa Wisener
Phil DeHaven
Eurby and Debbie Grubbs
Marsha Cockerill
Elaine Love
Sharon E. Smith

*Membership changed some throughout the multiyear project.

The Restorationists

Helen Wildermuth of Stonehugger Cemetery Restoration
Mark Davis of Stone Savers Cemetery Restoration

The Editors

Patricia Meeks Knasinski and Anne Moorman Riddle edited the content of the book in great detail, searching out my typos, spelling errors, non-sensible sentences, and all the other errors obvious to them when I believed it was nearly a finished product! They also made suggestions on making it better, clearer, or to simply flow better for the reader. I am so grateful to both for their hours of work. The book is better thanks to their involvement and interest.

A Few Words From the Author....

When I was growing up in Winchester, a kid over the age of three could play all up and down their street as long as they could see their house. From about six years on, you could ride your bike or scooter around the block. At about age nine you could ride all over your "end of town" as long as you checked in for meals and got home before the street lights came on. And it didn't matter what you were doing, everyone was watching you and reporting back to your Mom. If you misbehaved or broke the rules Mom would be waiting to mete out the punishment.

It was in this setting that a friend and I discovered the old graveyard out by the edge of our end of town, next to the National Guard Armory. We thought that no one else knew of its existence because it was overgrown with weeds taller than we were. But it was full of gravestones dating from the mid to late 1800's and we considered it our own special place. A bologna sandwich and a cookie were all we needed for a picnic at the graveyard, sitting among the weeds next to *Our Jonnnie's* gravestone. We were ten and eleven years old when we made our great discovery.

Our excitement subsided when school resumed and peaked again the next summer. But as we got older our interests changed and, except for an occasional visit, the graveyard was left to crumble away. I later learned that we were not alone. In fact, many people had an interest in the graveyard. Some people have told me that they loved playing there, others enjoyed visiting and reading the tombstones. Some even hoped that someday someone would come along and restore it. Others drove by many times, never knowing it was a cemetery.

After studying the history of the times, I learned that David Heaston gave the original land and later donated an addition. Its official name is the Heaston Cemetery, but after about 1880 when Fountain Park Cemetery was opened, it became known as the "Old Winchester Graveyard". Almost from the beginning local citizens were not pleased with the placement because the land had poor drainage and was a soggy place to bury loved ones. But it was Winchester's only burial ground from 1844-1880.

I found some newspaper articles about the graveyard by going through microfilm. Some of them help us learn about the history and about the cemetery's road to almost total destruction.

On August-18-1863, the following article appeared in the Winchester Journal: A group met about " putting a fence around the cemetery and improving the grounds". The named committee members were: Jacob Eltzroth Esq., Chair; H.H. Neff, Secretary; C.S. Goodrich, Esq.; Dr. A.F. Teal; and James Brown Esq. (Eltzroth, Goodrich and Dr. Teal's daughter are all buried in the graveyard.) Two hundred dollars was set aside with the rest of the needed money expected to be donated "by our citizens to enclose the cemetery with a good substantial fence." The article went on to say "We as citizens of Winchester and vicinity ought to feel a common interest in this matter, and make liberal donations, and otherwise aid in the prosecution of an enterprise that is so laudable and proper."

In 1876 there was a centennial remembrance at the cemetery. Soldier's graves were decorated, a band played, a choir sang and I.P.Watts delivered a speech.

On May-12-1880, following the opening of Fountain Park Cemetery, a newspaper item said "A movement is underway to secure a lot and remove the remains of soldiers from the old cemetery to the new one." To some extent history tells us that this happened because there are Civil War soldiers at Fountain Park, but many remain buried today in the Old Winchester.

There were several items about remains being moved to Fountain Park. One from 1-5-1887 stated: "Rachael Way had the remains of her husband, Henry T. Way, removed from the old and moved to the Fountain Park. The coffin was rotted away and there was little left but bones."

One article, not dated, said: "The remains of the father of W.P Needham, who died twenty-three years ago, were taken up yesterday and were found to be petrified. Several parties who knew the deceased in life very readily recognized the features."

In the Winchester paper of 5-25-1887 it was written: "How about cleaning up the old cemetery? Its condition is a disgrace upon civilization, fences down, gates standing wide open, the grounds overrun with weeds and briars. What is everybody's business is nobody's business and the cemetery is entirely neglected."

On 6-8-1887 someone wrote: "The Old Cemetery is a gloomy place in its present dilapidated condition; and as the Irishman said, we don't intend to be buried there as long as we live."

In more modern times, on July 4, 1956, an item in the newspaper mentioned that Mayor Ralph West, Sr. intended to clean up the cemetery and ask the public for donations. Then on July 5 an article mentioned that the mayor and a handful of interested citizens made a noticeable start on clearing away trees and brush from the Winchester burial ground on Western Ave. The article indicated that there was a Cemetery Fund and that the goal was to restore the cemetery completely and make it into a historical monument. There didn't seem to be much financial interest in the project and there was no further mention in either Winchester paper during the rest of 1956.

And so the years passed, the graveyard was neglected and the decay continued.

After getting my nursing education at Ball State and Ball Memorial Hospital, I moved to California where I spent most of my adult life. Each visit home would include at least one visit to the old graveyard. And each visit found it in worse condition, with most of the grave-stones gone, or under the ground, toppled and forgotten.

I moved back to Winchester in January, 2003. I stood in the snow in the graveyard and counted only seven standing gravestones. My first thought was "How could this have been allowed to happen?" But such thoughts are always a waste of time because one cannot change what is. So I changed my thought to "If enough people care, we can restore this place." That's when my restoration crusade began. I didn't know many people, nor did I know what to expect from the community, but I had the energy and passion to take on the project.

The response from the community was wonderful. People readily volunteered to be on the Restoration Committee, knowing it would be a several year project. Just to let you know what was involved, I will take you briefly through the steps. First, I studied the Indiana laws related to cemeteries, discovered that the Old Winchester met Indiana's definition of an abandoned cemetery, and that mowing and maintaining the grounds was the responsibility of the White River Township trustee. After explaining the goals to the trustee, the committee was given permission to restore the graveyard. The Randolph County Historical Society Board agreed to give validation to the project by making it one of their projects as long as it remained financially independent.

After outlining what needed to be done and developing a timeline, the work of fund- raising began. That involved talks to service organizations and any group willing to listen, letters and articles in the newspaper, requests to local foundations and other efforts. The result was incredible and almost all of the funding for the restoration was from donations. All of our goals were accomplished. Every gravestone that could be restored was put back together and reset. All, except a portion along the north side, had been fenced. It had been named a historical cemetery by the Indiana Department of Natural Resources. We developed a list of known burials, a list of those with restored gravestones, and a list of those whose remains were moved to Fountain Park Cemetery. We studied each of the soldiers buried there and ordered new markers from the Veteran's Administration. We believed that we had given Winchester back an important part of its history.

This book, however, is not intended to be about the restoration process, but rather a history of the people buried in the graveyard. There are three volumes of notebooks created by the restorationists and available for studying at the Randolph County Historical Society Museum. The notebooks contain before and after pictures along with the wording on each restored gravestone, including epitaphs.

Once the project was completed, the Restoration Committee celebrated by putting on a Rededication and Memorial Day Ceremony on May 17, 2009. It was based on Decoration Day ceremonies that took place at the graveyard in the 1870's. Music was provided by some Winchester Community High School band and choir members. Students from Driver Middle School History Club placed flowers on each gravesite. There were historical reenactments of five people buried in the graveyard, portrayed by Tom Franklin, Emily Goodrich Roberts, Gavin Craig, Bobby Manning and Gabe Winkle. Cindy Winkle portrayed a widow who placed a rose on the gravesite of a soldier. An honor guard from the Museum of the Soldier in

Portland, Indiana dressed in Civil War uniforms, gave a salute to the soldiers of the War of 1812 and the Civil War who are buried there. A cannon was fired and taps was played. The Master of Ceremonies for the event was Mayor Steve Croyle and the scripts were written by Sharon E. Smith.

Mission accomplished! Five years of dedication, donations, lots of research, and we had our graveyard back. But for me it just wasn't enough. The people buried there played such important roles in our history. So I began a two- plus year project of researching everyone on the list of known burials with the end goal of placing the information in a unique type of history book.

Anyone who engages in genealogy knows the frustration of names being spelled differently on census records and other documents. Dates are often inconsistent and confusing. You have to love being a detective when searching through old records. The intention is always to be as accurate as possible with a bit of "right place, right time" thrown into the mix. I spent over two years going through local records and reading virtually every local newspaper on microfilm for the years of the graveyard's active burial period. There is a great collection of census reports, marriage records, wills, probate records and family histories at the Randolph County Historical Society Museum. The collection of history books is also impressive. Monisa Wisener guided me to and through all of the resources, many of which she had personally collected through the years.

This book is full of data that could be helpful to a genealogist. The names and dates are as I found them on records. Spellings, dates and places are sometimes confusing, but anyone who does genealogy already knows that is part of the chase. Mr. Casey, my high school college grammar teacher, would be aghast at some of the vocabulary and grammar in the old newspapers, but I have included them in this book as written. I actually marveled at the accuracy, considering the work it took to put a newspaper together back then.

My main goal is to provide the reader with a history of Winchester through the experiences of the first white people to live here, to "bring them to life" by telling their stories. After completing most of the research, my Mother became ill and needed me, so the book was placed on a back burner until I could again focus on it. Mom passed away in December, 2012. Work restarted on this book in February, 2013. Just like taking care of Mom, this book has truly been a labor of love.

Chapter One

Indiana Pioneer Life

People came to Indiana from places east, at first as a trickle, then in ever-increasing numbers. They were old and young, mostly poor, looking for opportunity to own land and create prosperity for themselves and their families. Many Quakers came to get away from slavery, of which they strongly disapproved. Some were born in the United States while many others came from virtually every European country. Many from Germany settled in this area.

The journey from civilization to the forest home of Indiana was extremely difficult. The route lay, for the most part, through a rough country. It took many weeks for the travelers to reach their destination. Along the way they endured swamps, marshes, rivers to cross, dangerous forests with sometimes not so friendly Indians. They spent many a night sleeping on the ground.

Some had a roughly-made farm wagon for the women and youngest children to ride in, while the older children and men walked the entire distance. Even those blessed to have larger, sturdier wagons found the trip to be tedious, tiresome and sometimes dangerous. If someone died along the way, they would be buried in the forest and the journey would continue.

Indiana was a land of unbroken and thick forest. Settlers followed the Indian trails, usually along rivers. Once they reached their destination, the first order of necessity was to clear some land and build a cabin. Trees were felled with an ax and day by day the cabin grew. There was a chimney for cooking and usually one window and a door. Even though the pioneers lived isolated from each other they found those who lived within a few miles and communities were born. Pioneers tended to be a happy lot because they were pleased with their accomplishments and looked forward to a better and wealthier life.

Once the cabin was completed the work of clearing the land for agricultural purposes was started. This was no easy task either, with miles of dense forest in every direction, with creeks, rivers and small lakes scattered throughout the area. Everyone, including young children, became involved with the clearing of the land, followed by the planting, tending and harvesting of the crops, mostly corn. Mills were built along rivers so that the grains could be transported for sale in cities like Cincinnati, Ohio.

The pioneer boys and girls knew nothing of fine dress or the fashions of the day. Instead they wore hand- made clothing made from cloth intended to be durable, not fashionable. They spent their time behind a plow or using the wash tub along a brook or making cloth at the spinning wheel.

Because the pioneers came from so many different countries with so many different languages and customs, joining together was not always easy. But they all yearned for companionship and a common society. They set aside their own prejudices and joined together with their shared goals, thus becoming an organized society of sturdy, simple and affectionate people.

People helped each other, shared in their accomplishments and mourned together during their tragedies. They developed a social life that was not always work-related. For example, a wedding was always a fun time for the pioneer. They married young without the distinction of rank or fortune. The marriage was always held at the home of the bride, a merry journey on foot, horseback or by cart. Once the marriage ceremony was over, a dinner was served, followed by dancing and merriment that generally lasted until the next morning.

Following the wedding it was not unusual for everyone to get together and build the young couple a cabin of their own. Often this would only take one day with each person or team of people having their tasks to complete. This would be followed by a "warming" or dance full of spirit and hilarity.

Going to the mill in Cincinnati, Ohio was quite an undertaking which required two or three days. Some traveled on horseback with their bag of grain on the horse's back; others had a pair of oxen and a two-wheel cart. Flour was an essential for the pioneer family, so wives waited anxiously for the return of their husbands from the mill.

As the years passed toward the mid-1800's, cities began to grow and were joined together by railroads, which also carried the grain. Cabins were replaced by frame homes. Forests began to disappear and large open cornfields were seen throughout the countryside. Children were going to school, learning to play the piano and spending less time working with their parents. While the number one occupation was farming, there were now doctors, lawyers, carpenters, blacksmiths, teachers and all the other occupations needed for both rural and urban life. By the 1860's, the residents of Winchester were looking back at the first pioneers with the same gratitude that we give to them.

This movement of people into what was then the Indiana Territory began in the early 1800's. As previously stated, Indiana became a state in 1816, Randolph became a county in 1818, and Winchester was named the county seat the same year. Winchester was platted in 1818 by Paul Way and the first house was built in 1819. Growth was slow and no other towns were established in Randolph County for another ten years.

In reading Ebenezer Tucker's 1882 "History of Randolph County", it seems incredible that Mr. Tucker had the foresight to write this remarkable book. We are fortunate he did. It contains almost everything you might ever want to know about Randolph County and its communities, a must reference source for historians and genealogists.

Chapter Two

Illnesses and Life Expectancy: Mid 1800's

Death records were not generally kept until the late 1800's. It is therefore difficult to be very exact about the causes of death. However, many death notices and obituaries mentioned the cause of death, either by the name the doctor gave the family or by a description of the symptoms.

It is important to keep in mind that sanitary and housing conditions that existed during this time may have contributed to illness and death. Today the most common causes of death are chronic diseases such as heart disease, cancer and respiratory conditions. Deaths in the mid-1800's were more commonly caused by communicable diseases. Diseases with the shared symptoms of fever, chills, diarrhea and vomiting spread through families and communities. A child could go from healthy to dead in a day due to dehydration, which is believed to be the most common cause of death in babies and young children during those years.

If medical education and treatment of illnesses is of interest to you, I encourage you to go to the library or the internet for more information. I found many sources available. For this book I choose to give you some basic information and definitions so that when you read the obituaries included in the book you can interpret the meaning of the diagnoses named.

Of interest, the Department of Health and Human Services, National Center for Health Statistics, published a report in 2006 that compared life expectancy in the year 1850 to the year 2004. A white male baby born in 1850 could expect to live to be 38.3 years, a white female 40.5 years. If a white male lived to age 10, they could expect to live to be age 58, and a white female to age 57.2 years. Those white males who survived to age 20 could expect to live to be 60.1 years and white females to age 60.2.

In comparison, a white male born in 2004 can expect to live to be 75.7 years. If alive by age 10 he can expect to survive to age 76.3, and if alive at age 20 he can expect to reach 76.7 years. The statistics in this study are extensive and I only use these examples to give you some idea of life expectancy during the years that the Old Winchester Cemetery was being used for burials.

While epidemics of Cholera, Malaria, Diphtheria and Typhoid Fever spread throughout some areas of the United States in the late 1800's, I did not find that there were any such epidemics in Winchester during the period of 1820-1880. There were certainly deaths from these diseases, including several in a single family or community, but they did not reach epidemic proportions.

Following is a glossary of medical diagnoses and terminology used during the 1800's:

Cholera: An acute infection of the bowel with profuse watery diarrhea and vomiting, causing severe dehydration, usually caused by eating or drinking contaminated foods and drinks, sometimes called Dysentery on death notices.

Cholera Infantum: Summer diarrhea of infants, distinct from the cholera mentioned above, it was a non-contagious disease of young children who had been weaned from the breast, and occurred mainly between the months of April and October.

Malaria: Referred to as recurring chills and fever, charges fever, chill blains, chill fever, panama fever, swamp fever or the shakes. Its highest incidence was during the Civil War, causing the death of many soldiers, prevalent near marshy swampland where mosquitoes multiplied rapidly.

Diphtheria: Could occur any time of the year, but was more prevalent during the fall and winter months. The majority of cases occurred in children under age 10, it was highly contagious so could rapidly spread through families. The symptoms were similar to scarlet fever or croup.

Typhoid Fever: Marked by exhaustion, fever, headache and abdominal pain, it was mostly found in crowded unsanitary places, so that it was more common in army camps than in family homes. It was also referred to as bilious fever, camp fever, jail fever, hospital fever, putrid fever, ship fever or spotted fever.

Puerperal Fever: Also called child bed fever, metritis or purpura, death was caused by a bacterial infection during and after giving birth. It was considered to be a common and dreaded consequence of motherhood. In the 1800's it was second only to tuberculosis as the leading cause of death of women of childbearing age. If surgery was needed for childbirth it was performed by barber surgeons. Infant mortality for cesarean section was near 100%, usually taking the life of the mother as well. Hemorrhage post partum was also a frequent cause of death.

Tuberculosis: Called Consumption here in Winchester, it was also referred to as lung sickness, long sickness, white swelling, white plague or the wasting disease. One hundred years ago one in every seven people died of tuberculosis. The primary symptoms were cough, prolonged fevers, bloody sputum and general wasting of the body. Once diagnosed it was a slow death sentence.

Erysipelas: A contagious skin disease characterized by burning heat resulting from an acute inflammation of the skin, caused by the strep bacteria. It would begin as a very high fever, chilling and swelling of the face. Although it is listed as generally not fatal, I found it listed as the cause of death in several obituaries.

Dropsy: Today we call this congestive heart failure. The term generally referred to people who were swollen with water. It was also called anasarca, ascites, water retention or eclampsia.

Bright's disease: A general term used to mean death caused by some form of kidney failure. It was often seen in people who had previously has some sort of strep infection. Since there was no treatment for bacterial infections or for kidney failure, home remedies were the only available treatments. One common treatment of the time was drinking one's own urine. There is no significant data to suggest that this was effective.

Effluvia: In the mid-nineteenth century, these were commonly called "vapors", and were most frequently experienced by females. One of the sources I used for these definitions said that this illness was found especially in those of noxious or toxic character. I did not find this listed as a cause of death in anyone in the Old Graveyard but included it because even in the 1900's women "got the vapors," although I have never heard of anyone dying from it. Today we might call it hysteria.

Softening of the Brain: A term generally used to describe any disruption in the thinking process or in deterioration of the nervous system, It could be caused by a stroke, or a disease such as multiple sclerosis or Parkinson's disease. It was also referred to as old timer's disease or dementia.

Death from Teething: Before the discovery of antibiotics to treat infections and before adequate dentistry, people died from tooth infections. It didn't help that toothaches were commonly treated by cutting the gum to release the infection, usually with some non-sterile knife, thus complicating an already existing infection.

Epilepsy: Falling sickness, convulsions, fits or Jackson's March are all terms used for epilepsy in any of its forms.

The Grippe: Essentially the flu or influenza.

Lock Jaw: Now called tetanus, it is a bacterial infection causing neck and jaw stiffness. In its late stages it is difficult to open the jaw at all. It may be accompanied by body spasms.

Quinsy: A general term for tonsillitis.

Scarlet Fever: This was a major cause of death in children. It was caused by the strep bacteria and presented with a skin rash and a very high fever. Death from collapse of the circulatory system often occurred within 24-48 hours.

Measles: Another common disease that often led to death due to high fever and general malaise. Along with scarlet fever, this disease was highly contagious and spread rapidly through families and communities.

There are many sources for medical terminology of the 1800's. I have tried to limit the list of those diagnoses that often caused death and were mentioned in the obituaries of persons buried in the Old Winchester Graveyard.

Chapter Three

Known Burials in the Old Winchester (Heaston) Graveyard

It took several years to compile a list of persons who are known to be buried in the Old Winchester Graveyard. The list has 276 names. The plat of the cemetery indicates that about 1500 persons may be buried there. Unfortunately, many people are lost to history, so the unnamed are honored with a memorial marker at the entrance gate. The following resources were used to compile the list:

1. The book, <u>The History of Randolph County</u>, E. Tucker, 1882, listed people over the age of 65 known to be buried in all the cemeteries of Randolph County, including the Heaston. Mr. Tucker didn't want the settlers of the area forgotten.

2. Microfilm of old Winchester newspapers yielded 97 obituaries, many of them stating that the person was buried in the cemetery. Some were included because they died during the time that the Old Winchester was the only burial grounds in the city.

3. All the burial records from the Fountain Park Cemetery were reviewed for deaths occurring before 1880, the year it opened. Anyone buried there who died before 1880 had to have been moved from somewhere else. I compared those to the list being compiled for the Old Winchester and deleted

the names of persons who are documented as being moved to Fountain Park. One result was that I found some people with a gravestone in both cemeteries. This made sense because some families were concerned about the deterioration of the Old Winchester and wanted a lasting memorial at Fountain Park, even though the remains of their loved ones were left in the Old Winchester.

4. Some of those whose remains were moved from the Old Winchester to Fountain Park were reported in a local newspaper.

5. Those who had memorial markers recovered and restored were assumed to still be buried in the Old Winchester unless there was some record that their remains had been moved.

6. Some are on the list because they died between 1844-1880, lived in Winchester, and are not listed at Fountain Park Cemetery, White River Friends Church Cemetery or Maxville Cemetery.

Key:

R: restored memorial marker

C: fragments only, placed in cache (a common unmarked site at the graveyard)

K: known by history to be buried in the Old Winchester Graveyard but memorial marker not found

Totals: 276 known burials

157 restored gravestones, including partial stones with some information such as a name, date, initials and/or an epitaph. Footstones are counted but not included on this list.

Ages: Unknown   16   5.8%

       Newborn through age 17   89   32.2%

       Ages 18 through 87   171   62.0%

STATUS	NAME	BIRTH-DEATH	OBITUARY
R	Adams, Ephraim N.	1822-1858	
K	Aker, Melissa J.	1850-1875	yes
K	Alexander, Frances Ehart	1772-?	
K	Alexander, James	1769-?	
R	Alexander, Thornton	1809-1854	
R	Allen, Phillip	1795-1849	
R	Anthony, Iowa B.	1841-1874	yes
K	Avery, Mary D.	1833-1858	yes
R	Badgley, Rebecca*	1772-1859	
R	Bailey, David D.*	1828-1870	
K	Baldwin, Samuel A.*	1854-1877	yes
R	Beaty, Willie	?-1865	
K	Bell, Ellen	1842-1875	yes
R	Bennett, Catherine J.	1830-1854	
K	Best, Harry C.	1879-1880	yes
K	Beverly, Carolina Louisa	?-1853	
K	Beverly, Eldred	1851-1860	yes
K	Beverly, Iris	1861-1862	yes

K	Biggs, Alice Williams	?-1859	
K	Biggs, David	?-1872	
K	Biggs, Horace	1817-1884	yes
K	Biggs, James F.	1847-1882	
K	Biggs, Sarah A.	?	
K	Binson, Caleb	1847-1848	
R	Bolender, John	1790-1865	yes
K	Bolender, Mary Slammer	1794-1872	
R	Boyden, O.P., Rev.	1818-1865	
R	Bradbury, M.A.	1834-1875	yes
K	Brice, Infant	1875-1875	yes
R	Brown, Emily Charlene	1851-1853	
R	Brown, Laura	1847-1847	
R	Brown, Sarah	1797-1871	yes
R	Brown, Thomas	1792-1877	yes
R	Bunch, Infant	1860-1860	
R	Bunch, Rebecca	1823-1860	yes
R	Bunch, Thomas	1832-1860	
R	Bunch, Daughter	unreadable	
R	Bundy, Mary L.	1854-1854	
R	Bundy, Minerva E.	1833-1854	
K	Burke, Quintilla	1852-1873	yes
R	Burris, Thomas	1835-1857	

K	Burton, Edmund	1780-1865	
R	Burton, Esther	1796-1861	
R	Campbell, Hester	1803-1860	
K	Canada, Clarence W.	1886-1889	
R	Carter, Eliza E.	1843-1869	
R	Carter, James E.	1856-1856	
R	Carter, John D. "Our Jonnie"	1857-1862	
K	Chapman, William D.	1863-1883	yes
R	Churchman, F. Alexina	1853-1853	
R	Clark, Eliza Ann	1818-1859	
K	Clevenger, Infant	1875-1875	yes
K	Clevenger, Julie A.	1846-1883?	yes
K	Clevenger, Martha M.	1807-1875	yes
K	Colgrove, Harry Winfield	1879-1880	yes
R	Colgrove, Napoleon Bonaparte	1850-1866	
K	Colgrove, Wilford H.	1874-1875	yes
R	Condon, Patrick	1844-?	
K	Conner, Charles Theodore	1858-1860	yes
R	Conner, Caroline E.	1841-1861	yes
R	Conner, Lavina N.	1845-1868	
K	Cottom, David J.	?-?	
R	Cottom, Louisa Caroline	1854-1855	
K	Cottom, Nancy	1796-1867	yes

K	Cottom, William Sherman	1865-1856	
R	Craig, Susannah A.	1794-1864	
R	Demint, Brown***	1852-1853	
R	Dwyre, Mary	1855-1855	
K	Dye, Mr.	?-1839	
R	Edwards, Elizabeth*	1788-1863	
R	Edwards, Mary	?-1872	
R	Edwins, Stanley Walter	1862-1863	
R	Eltzroth, Elizabeth Neff	1796-1864	
K	Eltzroth, Jacob	1794-1871	yes
R	Eltzroth, James M.	1834-1859	
R	Eltzroth, Lewis C.	1835-1854	
R	Ennis, Emma Lee	1862-1863	
R	Ennis, Georgie W.	1864-1865	
R	Ennis, Isabella P.	1814-1865	
R	Evans, B.W.	1815-1886	
R	Evans, Mary E.*	1841-1879	yes
R	Evans, Tommy W.*	1877-1877	yes
K	Everetts, Arlie Owen	1876-1877	
R	Farra, Nancy	1821-1852	
K	Felt, Ella May	1880-1880	yes
R	Fie, Catherine	1787-1867	
K	Fitzpatrick, J. Harvey	1819-1873	yes

R	Ford, Martha	1815-1863	
K	Fox, Maria A.	1847-1877	yes
R	Frazer, Thomas	1836-1869	
R	Fulghum, J. Albert	1839-1870	yes
K	Gerstner, George G.	1809-1879	yes
K	Gerstner, Charlotte Greenawalt	1811-1867	
K	Gerstner, Charles	1854-1870	yes
R	Gillam, William H.	1856-1857	
K	Ginger, Albert F.	1847-1878	yes
R	Ginther, Henry	1866-1877	yes
K	Goodrich, Carey Seldon	1811-1865	
R	Goodrich, Emma Jane	1852-1860	
R	Goodrich, John H.	1847-1850	
K	Goodrich, Lydia Ann Hutton	1815-1869	
R	Goodrich, "Our Babe"	1865-1865	
K	Goodrich, Rebecca Pearse	1787-1867	yes
K	Goodrich, Thomas Watkins	1803-1839	
K	Gordon, Mary A.	1847-1873	yes
K	Groshong, Malinda "Belinda"	1821-1849	
R	Harrman, Frank	1850-1872	
R	Harrman, Hannah	1852-1855	
R	Harrman, Henry	1811-1880	yes
R	Harrman, Philippine	1809-1878	yes

K	Harvey, James W.	1812-1875	yes
K	Heaston, Catherine**	1791-1876	yes
K	Heaston, David**	1793-1865	yes
K	Heiks, Laura	?-?	
K	Hill, Lottie	1848-1876	yes
R	Hinson, Jacob	1837-1848	
R	Houk, Nancy E.	1830-1869	
K	Houser, James	?-?	
R	Hull, Elizabeth	1824-1853	
K	Hull, John Sr.	1766-1849	
R	Hull, J.R.*	1846-?	
K	Hull, Phebe	1773-1849	
R	Hull, William W.	1819-1851	
K	Humphries, Infant	1885-1885	yes
K	Huston, John	1784-1849	
K	Huston, Nancy	1793-1869	
K	Hutchens, Hannah Davis	?-?	
K	Hutchens, Josiah	1800-?	
K	Irvin, Mary Banty	1808-1843	
K	Irvin, Robert	1805-1875	
K	Jarrett, Carrie	1870-1873	yes
K	Jarrett, Baby	1873-1873	yes
R	Jarrett, Emily Charlene*	1843-1872	yes

K	Johnson, Edna Mae	1883-1883	
R	Jones, Harriett N.	1819-1873	yes
R	Jones, Thomas W.O.	1850-1864	
K	Jones, Thomas W.	1813-1867?	
K	Jones, Thomas W.	1869-1873	yes
R	Jones, Xerxes (X.A)	1839-pre-1873	
R	Kayser, Julia	1827-1878	yes
R	Keener, Aaron	1847-1873	yes
R	Keener, Catherine	1825-1895	yes
R	Keener, Jacob	1812-1884	
R	Keener, Nicholas	1815-1897	yes
K	Keller, Christian Franklin	1865-?	
K	Keller, Johan Heinrich	1861-?	
K	Keller, Maria	1860-?	
K	Keller, Rosina	1859-?	
R	Kelley, Jemima	1782-1855	
K	Kinney, Susanah	1860-1877	yes
R	Lavin, Sophie Martin	1840-1855	
C	Lavin, Infant	1855-1855	
K	Lavin, Michael	?-1872	yes
R	Lennon, Elizabeth	1859-1860	
R	Lewelling, William (Willie) E.	1868-1870	

R	M.I.	Stone found buried next to America McConochy, unreadable	
R	Mace, Cynthia	1833-1868	
R	Manderbach, Leo	1860-1862	
R	Martin, Elisha J.	1862-1868	
R	Martin, Elizabeth	1815-1874	
R	Martin, Elizabeth	1828-1852	
K	Martin, Joseph	1800-1871	yes
K	Martin, Male Child	?- 1876	
R	May, Jesse, Capt.	1836-1866	
R	McConochy, America	1838-1866	
K	McLeaf, Mr.	?-?	
K	Meier, Nora Charlotta	1880-1880	
K	Meier, Norwood Kar	1880-1880	
K	Miller, Mary Ann	1826-1879	yes
K	Miller, James	?-1873	
R	Miller, Sarah J.	1846-1861	yes
R	Monger, James K.	1844-1845	
R	Monger, Margaret	1828-1848	
R	Monger, Mary A.	1822-1841	
K	Monks, Belinda Hulitt	?- pre-1842	
K	Monks, Infant	Probably with mother, above	

K	Monks, George W.	1814-1865	
K	Monks, Mary Ann Irvin	?-1864	
K	Monks, John W.	?-1865	yes
R	Monks, Priscilla	1822-1861	
R	Monks, Walter Scott	1816-1873	
R	Monroe, A.D.C.	1823-1862	
K	Morrow, Mary Adella Bowen	?-1880	yes
R	Neff, Emily Charlene	1829-1860	
K	Neff, John Sr.	1770-1855	
K	Neff, Susan	?-1852	
K	Neff, Infant	?-?	
R	Page, Henraetta	1850-1854	
R	Page, William M.	1811-1865	yes
K	Page, Willard (Willie)	1859-1875	yes
R	Parker, Melvin	1832-1864	
R	Parker, Sarah E.	1830-1899	yes
K	Payne, Joseph	?-1876	
K	Payne, Rebecca Keener	1798-1880	yes
K	Payne, Susannah	?-1885	yes
R	Pettee, Amanda Jane	1848-1871	yes
K	Philps, Evaline Way	1839-1872	yes
K	Porter, Oscar	1858-1881	
K	Prather, Clifford H.	1870-1870	yes

K	Puckett, Baby	1873-1873	yes
K	Puckett, Bennie	1882-1884	yes
K	Puckett, Clida	1880-1882	yes
K	Puckett, Daughter	?-1881	
R	Puckett, Welcome G.	1801-1854	
R	Pullen, Oren E.	?-?	
K	Ramsey, David B.	1802-1864	
C	Ramsey, James	fragment, unable to read	
K	Ramsey, Maria	1781-1852	
R	Reece, Susannah	1776-1850	
R	Reed, Anna*	1808-1872	
R	Reed, Erastus H.*	1845-1864	yes
R	Reed, James E.*	1840-1857	yes
R	Reinheimer, Elizabeth F.	1860-1871	yes
K	Richards, Joseph	1860-1872	yes
R	Romaser, Andrew	1807-1850	
R	Romiser, Catherine	1851-1851	
R	Romiser, George W.	1849-1853	
R	Routh, Gertrude	1857-1858	
R	Routh, Sarah Elizabeth	?-1859	yes
R	Routh, Vianna	1855-1856	
R	Scott, Infant Helen	no dates	
K	Seagraves, Martin	1808-1875	yes

K	Segraves, Miss Jane	?-1872	yes
K	Segraves, Telitha K.	1843-1860	yes
R	Simpson, Susanna	1786-1855	
R	Smith, Cordelia S.	?-85?	
K	Smith, Edward	1863-1870	
K	Smith, Oliver P. "Coon"	?-1889	yes
R	Snyder, Catherine	1836-1879	
K	Soldier, Unknown	?-?	
R	Spencer, George E.	1853-1853	
R	Summers, Henry	1784-1871	yes
R	Summers, Susanna	1836-1853	
R	Teal, Dr. Asbury F.	?-1863	yes
R	Teal, Lillie Bell W.	1862-1863	
K	Towne, Nicholas J.	1790-1876	yes
R	Turner, James Ferris	1852-1853	
R	Turner, John R.	1819-1859	
K	Voris, Caroline	1850-1870	yes
R	Voris, Henry C.	1846-1868	
K	Voris, James R.	1852-1875	yes
R	Voris, Michael P.	1838-1872	yes
R	M.A.W., soldier, Civil War	?-?	
R	Way, Achsah Moorman	1786-1859	
R	Way, Infant	1862-1862	

R	Way, John	1778-1856	
K	Way, Mary Ann E.	1848-1876	yes
K	Way, Patience Green	1780-1858	yes
R	Way, Paul W.	1786-1856	
R	Way, Susanah	1820-1862	
K	Way, William M.	?-1839	
K	Way, Abigail	?-1829	

(The oldest of the Way family members who migrated here, William and Abigail were actually buried at the family farm. A memorial marker was placed in the graveyard by the family a few years later and was not found during restoration.)

K	Weaver, Mrs. Jacob	?-1880	yes
R	Welker, Martha Brown "Mattie"	1839-1890	yes
R	Welker, Squire	1829-1885	yes
R	Wells, four deceased children of Benjamin R. and Amelia		
K	Wells, Charles Quincy	1871-1872	yes
K	Wesp, Philibum	1869-1872	yes
K	Wilson, Miss Rebecca	1817-1880	yes
R	Woody, John Eberle	1840-1859	yes
K	Woody, Caroline	?-?	
R	Wright, Infant	1846-1846	
K	Wysong, David	1799-1878	yes
R	Wysong, Eliza Irvin	1807-1853	

*Have memorial markers in both the Old Winchester (Heaston) and the Fountain Park Cemeteries. The actual burial place is unknown.

** David and Catherine Heaston, who donated the land for the old graveyard, and after whom it is named, were known to have been buried in their cemetery. Their burial markers have not been found. There is a memorial marker in the Fountain Park Cemetery but no record of their remains having been moved. Their actual burial site is unknown but is believed to be somewhere in the Old Winchester.

*** Burial marker also in the Riverside Cemetery, Ridgeville, along with family members. The remains were probably not moved.

Several parts of gravestones were found that contained some information, but not enough to identify the person. They are listed here in case it may be helpful to someone seeking the gravesite of some ancestor. All information found on the partial stones is included.

STATUS	NAME	BIRTH-DEATH	AGE
R	Unknown, Unknown (found with Cordelia Smith)	1831-1853	22 y 22d
R	Unknown, Unknown	?-1854	23y 4m 15d
R	Unknown, Carolina	?-?	22 y 10m 16d
R	Unknown, Cordelia	?-?	?
R	Unknown, Curtie	?-?	?
R	Unknown, Joseph	?-?	?
R	Unknown, Unknown	?-1860	20y 6m 16d

R	Unknown, Unknown	?-1853	4m
R	Unknown, Unknown	?-1865	36y 2m 6d
C	Unknown, Unknown	no information	
C	Unknown, Unknown	partial epitaph "Life is short"	
R	Unknown, Unknown	?-1840	25y

Soldiers in the Old Winchester Graveyard

NAME	SERVICE	WAR
Bolender, John	French grenadier	Napoleonic
Boyden, O.P., Rev	Chaplain, 75th Indiana	Civil
Condon, Patrick	Co. E, 60th Ohio	Civil
Fulghum, J. Albert	Co. G, 106th Indiana Infantry	Civil
Heaston, David	Western frontier	War of 1812
Hull, J.R.	Co.A, 134h Indiana Infantry	Civil
Jones, Xerxes	Co. H, 84th Indiana	Civil
May, Jesse, Capt.	Co. B, 8th Indiana	Civil
Monks, Walter Scott	Co. B, 108th Indiana	Civil
Parker, Melvin	Co. H, 39th Iowa	Civil
Reed, Erastus H.	Co. F, 134th Reg, Indiana	Civil
Unknown	Listed in Tucker's History	Civil
Towne, Nicholas J.		War of 1812

Voris, Henry C.	Co. G, 8th Indiana, musician	Civil
Voris, Michael, 2nd Lt.	Co. G, 8th Indiana	Civil
M.A W.		Civil
Way, John	South Carolina	War of 1812
Welker, Squire	Co. H, 84th Indiana	Civil

CHAPTER FOUR

MEET THE PEOPLE BURIED IN THE OLD WINCHESTER GRAVEYARD

The next few chapters are intended to provide the reader with information about each person known to be buried in the Old Winchester Graveyard. For some people I was able to find lots of information, for others no information. It was not my intent to complete a genealogy study of each person, but I did hope to find something about each one. In some cases I did not succeed. If I found a death announcement or obituary on newspaper microfilm I include it here. If you want to know exactly what is written on each restored gravestone I invite you to take a tour of the cemetery, or go through the notebooks available at the Randolph County Historical Museum that were completed by the restorationists. The names are in alphabetical order.

Those who are on the list with initials or footstones only or who are listed as unknown are not included in these chapters. They are on the list because some part of their gravestone was found and could be important to a genealogist searching for an ancestor in the graveyard.

Some of the biographical data is presented in first person. Included are Jonnie Carter, Rebecca Pearse Goodrich, Melvin Parker, William Page and Paul Way. Others have longer, more extensive presentations because of their prominence and contribution to the founding of Winchester or because they have interesting stories. Those include: John Bolender, the Silas Colgrove Family, David and Catherine

Heaston, the Monks Family, the Nathan Reed family and the David Wysong Family.

It is helpful to keep in mind that some people who are in the graveyard may have been passing through the area on their way further west when they died of accident or disease. They would not be recorded on a census report or other document since census taking was done every ten years. That may account for finding nothing about them. It was frustrating, however, that there were some people who clearly lived in Winchester and had family here, but I still could not find them on any records. Perhaps they were missed by census takers, or chose to be obscure.

People visit cemeteries for a lot of different and personal reasons. For genealogists who are forever looking for their most elusive lost relative, old cemeteries are the most wonderful places in the world! For me, it's all about history. Even as a child I could look at a gravestone, read the name and dates and perhaps the epitaph, and sit quietly by the stone with all kinds of questions going through my head. What were they like? What caused them to die? Who was in their family? What was their house like?

By age 10, I came to think of some of the people buried in the old cemetery almost as friends. They had lived and loved and suffered and hurt and struggled and laughed and worked. I was fascinated that the people buried there were the first white people to come to what is now Winchester. They actually saw Indians and lived among them. They lived in a total wilderness and worked by hand to make a cabin or house and to clear fields so they could plant. They created a society, and wrote laws about how people should behave toward each other. They developed businesses because there was a need, and the need was met because they could. They only had themselves and their friends and neighbors to depend on. But they were living in a young and wonderful country where they had the freedom to fulfill their dreams. And they did.

CHAPTER FIVE

ADAMS, EPHRAIM N.-CARTER, JAMES E.

Adams, Ephraim N.   b 3 Jul 1822   d 21 Dec 1858   36y 5m 18d

Ephraim's memorial marker was found and restored. The only information I was able to find on him was that he was the father of Amanda J. Pettee, also buried here. I could not find him on any census, even on ancestry.com.

Aker, Melissa J.   b ? 1851   d 7 Apr 1875   24y

On the 1870 census of Winchester, Melissa, age 19, is married to John W. Aker, age 21, and they have a baby, aged 10 months named Charles F. Aker. John is listed as being a teamster. Looking back further I found Melissa J. as a 9 year old on the 1860 census of River Forest, Randolph County, living with her family. Her father was Jacob Edwards, age 33 and a farmer. Her mother was Catharine, age 25. She had siblings, Benjamin B., age 10, Elisabeth, age 8, Isaac, age 7 and William, age 5. I also found her husband, John, at age 12, living with his family in the same area. John's father was Andrew J, a farmer. His mother was Lucinda, age 38. John's siblings were David, age 8, Jacob, age 5 and Lauretta, age 2.

Death Notice: Winchester Journal, April 7, 1875

"At the residence of A.J. Aker in this place this morning, Melissa Aker, wife of John Aker. Funeral services tomorrow at 2 o'clock P.M. at Friends Church. All are invited to attend."

I then found a marriage record for John W. Aker to Emiling Eltzroth on December 30, 1875 by Min. R.S. Hagerman. It was not unusual for a husband to remarry soon after the death of his spouse, especially if he had young children to raise.

On the 1880 census of White River Township, Randolph County, John is 32 and a pump dealer, married to Emma, age 21, with children Charley, age 10, Clide ,age 2 and Myrtie, age 8 months.

Obituary: Winchester Journal, July 30, 1903

"John Aker died at the County Infirmary Mon morning and was buried at Fountain Park Cemetery Tuesday afternoon. He was taken to the Infirmary some time ago owing to his mental derangement. He was fifty years old and the son of Andrew Aker, who is eighty years old. He is the brother of David and Jady Aker and Mrs. Laura Bush."

Alexander, Frances Ehart   b 26 Sep 1772   d ? before 1875

Alexander, James   b 1769   d ? before 1850

James and Frances moved to Randolph County from Orange County, Virginia. Information about this couple is from the diary of one of their sons, Horace Martin Alexander, while he was on a mission as a member of the Mormon Church, during 1875 and 1876. He lists James and Frances's children as follows: William E. born 1793,

Adam E. born 1795, Fanney born 1798, Willis born 1800, Malinda born 1803, James A. born 1805, Thornton born 1809 and Horace Martin born 1812.

Horace also wrote in his diary:"returned to Winchester on the 25th of March (1876). Visited the graves of my father and mother, and brothers, and dedicated them to the Lord to wait the resurrection of the just."

The only cemetery in Winchester at the time was the Old Winchester, and we know for sure that Thornton is buried there. I believe that James and Frances are buried there also, along with at least one of Horace's brothers, but the only gravestone we found was for Thornton. (We were able to find and restore all or part of only 157 gravestones, even though we know that hundreds of people are buried in the graveyard.)

There is a family tree on ancestry.com about this family.

Alexander, Thornton   b 26 Nov 1809   d 28 Mar 1854   45y 4m 2d

Thornton married Eliza Hulett December 22, 1836 in Winchester. She was born 28 May 1819 in Vermont. Thornton is first found on the Winchester census in 1840. Individual names were not put on census reports until 1850, so in 1840 Thornton is listed as head of family consisting of a male between age 30-40 (Thornton), a male between age 70-80 (probably his father, James), a female age 20-30 (Eliza) and a female age 60-70 (probably his mother, Frances). There are no children listed.

On the 1850 census of Winchester, Thornton is listed as a trader. His mother, Frances, is 70 and living with the family. His father, James is no longer there and is probably deceased. Also listed are the following children of Thornton and Eliza: Horace, age 10, George W., age 8, Willis M., age 6, and Francis A., age 2.

Thornton was a prominent man in the community very early in Winchester's existence. In fact, he voted to incorporate Winchester as a town in 1838. As early as 1836 he held a grocer's bond. And at some point he also became the sheriff of Randolph County. He was a good friend and neighbor of a man named William Page, who owned a grocery and a groggery (sold liquor) and Thornton became one of his best customers. Thornton went on to become an alcoholic who sold most of his family's belongings to buy alcohol. The final blow was when he sold his wife's milk cow and featherbed, leaving his family destitute. (Of interest, at that time, men owned everything with the exception of a featherbed and a cow, those always belonging to the wife. This often shows up in old wills.) Thornton died of delirium tremons at the age of 45 when he no longer was able to buy alcohol to satisfy his addiction. Immediately after he died, his widow, Eliza, and about 80 women of Winchester stormed the groggery of William Page and smashed in all of the barrels of liquor and spilled them on the street. The story about that gets very exciting and will be told in its entirety when we get to William Page's story on page 163. Thornton and William are also neighbors in the Old Winchester Graveyard.

Eliza remarried and moved with her new husband, Robert Younter, and children to Illinois.

Allen, Phillip   b 16 Mar 1798   d 5 Aug 1849   51y 4m 19d

Phillip married Christine Oller on December 1, 1819 in Washington County, Pennsylvania. They are listed on the 1840 census of White River Township. He is listed as being a cabinet maker, and they have 11 children living in their household. By the 1850 census Christina is head of household and a widow, age 51, living in White River Township with children, John age 12, Abigail age 10 and Ellen age 6.

I was not able to find any further information about this family. There is some brief genealogy information on ancestry.com.

Anthony, Iowa　　　　b 1831　　　　d 23 Jul 1874　　　　32y 5m 7d

There is a marriage record for Thomas W. Anthony and Iona D. O'Neal in Randolph County for August 16, 1860. Then on the 1870 census for Winchester Thomas W. is 32 with no occupation listed, Iowa is 28 and there is a daughter, Ida, age 8.

Obituary, Winchester Journal, July 29, 1874

> "DIED_ At the residence of S. B. Bradbury, on Thursday evening last, Mrs. IOWA B. ANTHONY, in her 33rd year. The deceased was a sister of Mrs. Bradbury and was a most estimable lady. She leaves one little daughter, who will find a comfortable and happy home with Mr. Bradbury."

It is unknown what happened to her husband, Thomas, since he is not mentioned in her obituary and I was unable to find anything about him after 1870. Iowa had a sister, Margaret A. Bradbury living in Winchester, the wife of the Mr. Bradbury mentioned in her obituary. On the 1870 census their mother, Caroline Willets, lived with Margaret and Samuel Bradbury.

On the 1880 census their daughter, Ida, is living with her grandmother, Caroline Willits in Winchester. Ida became a seamstress and on August 20, 1881 married Charles Clingerman in Winchester.

Avery, Mary D.　　　　b ?　　　　d 5 Sep 1858　　　　25y

Death notice, Winchester newspaper:

> "DIED__At her residence in Winchester, September 5, 1858, Mary D. Avery, wife of C.A. Avery, in the 25th year of her age.."

The only other information I found was in 1864 C. A. Avery was listed on an excise tax list with a valuation of $825 and tax due of $41.25.

Badgley, Rebecca   b 11 Dec 1777   d 9 Feb 1859   86y 1m 29d

Rebecca was the wife of William, who died 11 Nov 1825 and was buried at the First Presbyterian Church cemetery in Elizabethtown, New Jersey. At some time after 1850 Rebecca moved to Winchester to live with a son, Joseph, and his wife, Abigail.

According to records of the Fountain Park Cemetery her remains were said to have been moved to Lot 45, Sec 7. However, a large and beautiful gravestone was found and restored in the Old Winchester Graveyard. Since the location of her remains is unknown, she is listed in both cemeteries.

Also on the Fountain Park burial list in the same burial site are Joseph (her son), Abigail (his wife) and Edmund and Elizabeth Carter (unknown relationship). All four are listed as having been moved from the old cemetery.

Her maiden name was Abbott according to genealogy records found at ancestry.com.

Bailey, David D.   b 12 Feb 1828   d 17 Feb 1870   42y 5d

I was unable to find any records on Mr. Bailey in Randolph County or on census records.

Baldwin, Samuel   b 1854   d 9 Mar 1877   23y 2m 7d

I found Samuel with his birth family on the 1860 census, New Garden, Wayne County, Indiana. He is listed as living with a mother whose name I could not read, age 32 and siblings, Meriam, age 14, Lydia, age 10 and John W., age 8.

Obituary, Winchester Journal, March 14, 1877:

" Died in this city, on Friday, March 9, 1877, of inflammation of the bowels, SAMUEL A. BALDWIN, age 23 years, 2 months and 7 days. The deceased was born near Jonesboro, Grant Co., Ind, and was an unusually bright baby. When eighteen months old, the day following his father's funeral, while playing around where his mother was washing, he fell backwards over one of the wash tubs, injuring his spine so severely that he was never able to walk afterward. His mind, however, was bright and for several years he had been in business being the senior member of the firm of Baldwin & O'Harra at the time of his death. Notwithstanding his afflictions, he was always in fine spirits, bright and cheerful at all times; and to know him was to be his friend. Among the many ingenious schemes to amuse himself and get about without the aid of others, he trained a pair of goats to pull his wagon, and for months nothing in Winchester attracted more attention than Sammy and his goat team, and when the weather was favorable, he was out, as proud and happy as a king. He also had a chair for getting about the house.

His sickness was of short duration, but he suffered great pain. He was at Richmond on Monday of last week and was taken sick the next day. He gave testimony that all was well with him and expressed no regrets at parting with his frail tenement of clay. He leaves a mother, two sisters and many friends to mourn his absence, but they mourn not as those without hope, knowing that the parting is of short duration."

Beaty, Willie   b ?   d 2 Mar 1865   ?

His tombstone says that he is the son of R. & E. I am assuming he was a baby or young child because of a lamb motif on his gravestone. I was unable to find any information about a family researching the R. & E. initials.

Bell, Ellen   b 1842   d 15 Apr 1875   33y

Death notice, Winchester Journal:

> "DIED__In this city on Thursday, 15th of April, Mrs. Ellen Bell, wife of Hiram Bell. She leaves besides her husband and friends, a family of six children to mourn their loss."

The family was found on the 1870 census in Washington Township, Wayne Co., Indiana. Hiram was 39 and a boot and shoe maker, Ellen was listed as age 28. The children were Ellen, age 10, Laura, age 8, Mollie, age 6, George, age 3 and Edwin, age 7 months. She must have had another child before her death five years later. Also living with the family was Anna Bell, age 71, probably the mother of Hiram.

Bennett, Catherine J.   b 1830   d 26 Nov 1854   24y 9m 24d

I was unable to find any information about this young lady. There were no names or initials on her tombstone to give any hint of her maiden name or her husband's name (if she was married).

Benson, Caleb   b 1847   d 2 Feb 1848   11m

On Caleb's tombstone he is listed as the son of Elijah and L. I searched through local records as well as at ancestry.com under the names Benson and Binson, but found no family information.

Best, Harry C.   1879   d ? May1880   1y 5m 2d

Obituary, Winchester Journal, May, 5,1880

"DIED__On Thursday morning last, Harry C., son of James M. and Lydia M Best, aged 1 year, 5 months and 2 days. Funeral services were held by Rev. R.D. Spellman last Friday, after which the body of little Harry was laid to rest in the old cemetery."

His parents, James M. Best and Lydia M. Thornhill were married in Randolph County sometime around March3, 1875 by Rev. Henry Merrill.

James M. Best's father, Thomas, started a grocery store in Winchester in 1867. James took it over, and then his son, Ed in 1913. There is a folder at the Randolph Country Historical Society Museum that has great information about the family and their business, J.M. Best and Son Grocery.

Beverly, Carolina Louisa Goodrich   b ?   d 1853   ?y

Carolina was the first wife of Dr. J.E. Beverly and the daughter of John Baldwin Goodrich and Rebecca Pearce Goodrich. Carolina and John E. were married July 20, 1843. They had two sons, John E. and Eldred.

After Carolina died her husband married her sister, AnnEliza Goodrich and they had three daughters, Rebecca, Eva and Iris Dr. Beverly died in Winchester May 6, 1888 and is buried at Fountain Park.

Carolina and her sister, Ann, are included in the information about their mother, Rebecca Pearce Goodrich, who is also buried in the Old Winchester Graveyard. Rebecca came to Winchester after her husband was killed in an accident in Virginia. She and her children were the beginning of one of the best known and most successful families of Winchester.

Beverly, Eldred   b 1851   d 30 Sep 1860   9y 3m 24 d

Obituary, Winchester Journal

"DIED__On Saturday, the 30th ult., of injuries received from the passage of a wagon over his body, Eldred, youngest son of Dr. J.E. Beverly, aged 9 years, 3 months and 24 days.

The circumstances that led to this afflicting casualty are briefly these: the father of the unfortunate boy was removing some loose top dirt from an alley that he was having graded to the interior of the premises to fill up some depressions in the surface. It was by the merest accident that the work was engaged. The oxen and wagon with which the hauling about the premises had been done through the season and were standing idle for want of the usual help, and it struck the father to clear away this dirt in order to plow portions of the ground again, an operation he wanted to do or superintend himself to get it to the proper depth. The elder brother of the deceased had driven in the first load when he left to do some errand at a nearby neighbors when the second lead was ready to start and the youngest boy started to drive it round. His father did not think of his getting on the wagon for so short a distance, but observing him to do so opposed no objection as he was like most boys, fond of riding and no thought of danger was entertained, the oxen being an old, thoroughly trained and tractable pair. Turning around the corner towards the place of entrance he went to jump from the wagon the better to guide the oxen in. As they walked slowly he did not take the precautions to stop them and by some slip or misstep fell to the ground just in front of the four- wheel which struck and passed over him before he could get out of the way. This so stunned and disabled him that he was unable to avoid the hind one which also passed over him about the middle of the abdomen probably inflicting the fatal injury. It happened that no one was observing him at the time, the house intervening between him and where his father was coming through the garden. His brother came from across the street and found him lying on the ground and insensible. The wagon was standing still immediately beyond him. On attempting to assist him he immediately got up himself and walked some ten steps to the fence where his father met him and took him into the house.

Finding no external marks of violence of any consequence and that he had so complete control of all his limbs and muscles his afflicted parents and friends ventured to hope that the injury might not be fatal. Their hopes, however, had soon to be given up, as after hours of intense suffering he began to exhibit signs of sinking , as it might be from internal hemorrhage and finally ceased to breathe about 12 hours after the accident. He was very amiable, and intelligent, respected and beloved by all who knew him."

Eldred was the youngest son of Dr. John E. Beverly and Carolina Louisa (deceased, see above). Dr. John was the son of Mary Way and Benjamin Beverly. Mary was the daughter of William Way, a brother of Paul Way, two of the earliest Winchester pioneers.

Beverly, Iris   b 1861   d 7 Nov 1862   1y 6m 11d

Death Notice, Winchester Journal, November 7, 1862:

"DIED__On the morning of the 5th inst., IRIS, infant daughter of Dr. J.E. Beverly, aged 1year, 6 months and 11 days."

Biggs, Alice Williams   b ?   d 1859   37y

First wife of Horace P. Biggs, she is found on the 1850 census in Preble County, Ohio, with her husband, Horace, age 38 and a weaver. Alice is 28 and their children are David L., age 8, John W., age 6 and James F. ,age 3.

Biggs, David   b 1842   d 19 Nov 1872   30 y

Obituary, Winchester Journal, November 20, 1872:

"DIED__In this city, on Monday evening last, of consumption, DAVID BIGGS, son of Horace P. Biggs and Alice (deceased). The deceased had been afflicted for several months, and death was to him a welcome release from his sufferings. He was a quiet, unobtrusive and worthy young man, strictly upright in his intercourse with his fellow men. His last words to his weeping friends were 'don't weep, I am not lost, but gone before.'"

Biggs, Horace P.   b 13 Mar 1817   d 6 Sep 1884   67y 5m 23d

Horace is mentioned above in the notice about his first wife, Alice, and they were in Preble County, Ohio on the 1850 census. While I could not locate them on the 1860 census, they were living in Winchester by that time. On the 1870 census, Horace is 54, living with Sarah Biggs age 27, David age 27 and James F. age 22, a tanner. On the 1880 census Horace is listed with James age 33 and Mary T. Biggs, age 16. James is shown on each census to be living with his father, so it appears he did not marry and have a family. On the 1880 census there was a question about health problems and James is listed as having bronchitis and Horace is listed with a broken arm.

Obituary, September 10, 1884:

"Horace P. Biggs was born near Elizabethtown Pa., March 13, 1817 and died in Winchester, Indiana, Saturday, September 6, 1884 at 8 a.m.; aged 67 years, 5 months and 23 days. In early life he removed to Columbiana County, Ohio, where he was married December 2, 1839 to Alice C. Williams, with whom he lived until her death in 1859. He was thrice married subsequently, the last time to Maria C. Stephens in 1882. He was the father of seven children, all of whom he was called upon to lay away in the silent rooms of the dead.

He joined the Methodist Episcopal Church in early life, and remained a consistent member until the time of his death. Though often deprived of the privilege of attending the means of grace by reason of affliction, his heart remained warm and tender, and he loved to speak of the religious training given him by his mother. His last expression concerning his spiritual condition was that he had taken comfort from the words of the Saviour in which he says 'Come unto me all ye that labor and are heavy burdened and I will give you rest.' The funeral services were conducted by Rev. J.C. Murray at the family residence on Sunday, at 4 p.m., and were largely attended."

In Horace's obituary it states that he had a total of seven children and all died before him, but I did not find any death notice for James. I am sure he is buried in the Old Winchester with the rest of the family. I also did not find the names of any children except for David, John and James on any census reports. They may have been born and died as children between census reports. I also don't know what happened to his last wife, Maria.

Biggs, Sarah A.   b 1843   d 1877   34 y

Sarah was a wife of Horace P., probably his second wife. I did not find any other information about Sarah.

Bolender,   b 12 Dec 1790   d 9 Dec 1865   74y 11m 27d
(Bolander, Bolinger), John (Johann)

John was born in Lower Hess, Germany. He came to the United States in July of 1834 with his wife, Anna Maria Schlemmer. They were married in Germany March 4, 1823. He is listed on the 1840 census of Randolph County as head of household between age 50-60, with a female between age 50-60 (his wife, now called Mary), a female between 15-20, a male between 10-15 and a female between 0-5. On the 1850 census of White River Township, Randolph County, John is listed as age 60 and a farmer. Mary is 56 and son Lewis is 25. Living in the same household, or next door (the census is not clear) are John's brother, George, along with his wife Christina and three children, Frederick age 18, Mary age 15 and Lewis age 6.

Randolph County, Indiana Civil Order Book 6, page 221: Naturalization papers filed and recorded March 20, 1840, Randolph Circuit Court, George W. Monks, Court Clerk:

"I, John Bolender, an alien, do make the following report of myself and declaration of intention of becoming a citizen of the United States, to wit; I am a native of the province of Lower Hess,, in Germany and was born on the 12th day of December, A.D. 1790 being now about fifty five years of age, immigrated from Bremen sometime in July, 1834 and landed at Baltimore in Maryland sometime in August of the same year, and settled in Franklin County, Pennsylvania, where I resided about eighteen months, and about the first of April, 1836 I removed to Richmond, Wayne County, Indiana then to Randolph County where I have lived ever since. And I declare that it is bona fide my intention to become a citizen of the United States of America and of the State of Indiana, and to renounce forever all allegiance and fidelity to any foreign prince potentate or state of Sovereignty whatever and particularly to William the second, Grand Duke of Fulda in Germany of whom I am now a subject."

Signed John Bolender and written in German.

May Term, A.D. 1846, Probate Order Book 6, page 243

"Be it remembered that at a Probate Court of Randolph County, held at the Court House in Winchester, Randolph County, Indiana in the United States of America, on the Eleventh day of May in the year of our Lord, one thousand eight hundred and forty-six, John Bolinger, a native of the kingdom Germany, exhibited a petition praying to be admitted to become a citizen of the United States and in appearing to the said Court that he had declared on oath before the Clerk of the Randolph Circuit Court, on the 20th day of March, A.D. 1844, that it was a bona fide his intentions to become a citizen of the United States and to renounce forever all allegiance and fidelity to any foreign dukes, potentates, State or Sovereignty, whatever and particularly to William the second Grand Duke of Fulda, of Germany, of whom he was at the time a subject and the said John Bolinger having on his solemn oath declared and also gave proof thereof by competent testimony of David Heaston and George W. Monks, two citizens of the United States, that he has resided one year and upward within the State of Indiana and within the United States of America as forward of five years immediately preceding his application and it appearing to the satisfaction of the Court that during that time, he has behaved as a man of good moral character attached to the principles of the Constitution of the United States and well disposed to the good…and happiness of the same and having on his solemn oath declared before the said Court that he did absolutely and would support the Constitution of the United States, and that he does hereby renounce and relinquish any title or order of nobility to which he was or hereafter may be entitled and that he does absolutely and entirely renounce any and all allegiance and fidelity to any foreign potentate, State and sovereignty whatever and particularly to William the second Grand Duke of Fulda of Germany, of whom he was last a subject. Therefore the court admitted the said John Bolinger to become a citizen of the United States and ordered that all the proceedings aforesaid be recorded by the Clerk of the said County which was done accordingly."

His brother, George, made the same oaths on the same day.

John is such a great example of what happened to someone who came to the United States from Europe speaking a language other than English. His German name, Johann Bolender was changed through the years to Bolander and Bolinger, and his descendents spell their names all three ways. Johann became John. His wife, Anna Maria Schlemmer became Mary, with the same confusion about her last name. On his tombstone he is John Bolender. In his wife's obituary her name is given as Mary Bolander (Slammer).

There is more confusion about John than just the spelling of his name. On his tombstone it says that he "served 6 years as a grenadier, a part of the time in the service against Napoleon Bonaparte". Tucker's History of Randolph County gives two contradictory accounts of John's military service in Germany.

On page 286 in the section on soldiers buried on Randolph County it states "John Bolander served six years as a grenadier, 3 years in active service against Napoleon Bonaparte." Then on page 346 Tucker writes "John Bolendar was in the French Army under Bonaparte, and was actively engaged in the battle of Waterloo. He also made the celebrated passage across the Alps with the French Army." One of John's descendents spent several years researching the family and his writings seem to conclude that John served with Bonaparte. It is this kind of contradiction that makes history so interesting and sometimes so confusing!

In Tucker's history book he also had biographical sketches and illustrations. One of his biographies was about a son of John and Mary named Lewis. It states that Lewis Bolander, a farmer, was born in the State of Hesse, Germany, November 12, 1826, the son of John and Mary (Slammer) Bolander and that he is the second of five children. Lewis was seven when he came to the United States. Three of the children were born in Germany and two in the United States. Of the five, two were living when the book was written in 1882, Lewis and a sister, Malinda Strohm, who was living at the time in St. Louis County, Missouri. The article also states that John entered land in White River township about 1836, cleared the land for a farm and that Lewis inherited the farm by will. I was unable to learn the names of the three deceased children of John and Mary or when they died or where they are buried.

Bolander, Mary Slammer   b 1794 ?   d 7 Jan 1872   78 y

As mentioned with the information about her husband, John, Mary's German name was Anna Maria Schlemmer. In the United States she became Mary with her last name spelled Slammer or Slamer.

Obituary, Winchester Journal, Jan, 10, 1872:

"DIED__Mrs. Mary Bolinger, a highly respected German lady died at the residence of her son, Lewis Bolinger, three miles southwest of this city, on Sunday morning last, in the 78th year of her age. Services were held at the German Church yesterday, after which the remains were interred in the cemetery."

Notice, Winchester Journal, Jan, 17, 1872:

"Errata__It was Mary Bolander whose death occurred on Sunday morning of last week, and not Bolinger, as the types made us say last week. There are Bolingers and Bolanders both living in the county, and in the hurry of writing our article we got the wrong names."(It was confusing even then!)

Boyden, O.B., Rev. b 1818 d 22 Aug 1865 47y

Orville B. Boyden was married to Bethiah Miller in Randolph County on April 8, 1846.

On the 1850 census Orville is 31 and a clergyman, Bethiah is 23 and they have Francis, age 2. On the 1860 census Orville is 41, a clergyman, Bethiah is 32, Francis is 12 and Bilber is 9.

Orville was a chaplain with the 75th Indiana during the Civil War. He enlisted as a private on August 1, 1862 at the age of 43. He transferred on October 14, 1862 from company E to company S. He was promoted to full chaplain on October 14, 1862 and resigned Co. S Infantry Indiana on February 15, 1863. Orville was discharged with distinguished service.

Bradbury, Margaret A. b 1833 d 12 Jun 1875 41y 11m 9d

Margaret was the wife of Samuel B. Bradbury and the sister of Iowa Anthony, previously listed, who share the same gravestone.

On the 1870 census of Winchester, Samuel is 38, Margaret is 36, Walter O. is 15 and Edward A. is 13. Caroline Willets is also living in the home. She is the mother of Margaret and Iowa Anthony.

Obituary, Winchester Journal, June 16, 1875:

"Died at her home in Winchester, Saturday morning last, June 12, 1875, MARGARET A. BRADBURY, wife of S. B. Bradbury, aged 41 years, 11 months and 9 days. Mrs. Bradbury had been in delicate health for several years past, and for the past five months had been entirely confined to her bed. She was born in Centerville in this state in 1833 and was married to Mr. Bradbury in 1852. She had resided in our town for several years, and by her rare social qualities and kindly disposition had won many warm friends. She was warm and steadfast in her attachments to her friends, and for her family her love was almost idolatrous. She leaves a husband, two sons, an aged mother, an orphan niece and many other relatives to mourn her early death. The remains were interred in the cemetery on Sabbath afternoon in the presence of one of the largest concourses of people we ever saw in Winchester on such an occasion."

Advertisement, Winchester Journal, March 14, 1877:

"I am just now receiving my stock of Spring Boots and Shoes. S. B. Bradbury"

Brice, Infant   b 1875   d 15 Jun 1875   4m

Obituary, Winchester Journal, June 23, 1875:

"A little four months old babe of N.R. Brice's died in Covington, Kentucky on Tuesday of last week. His remains were brought here for interment on Wednesday."

On the 1870 census of Winchester, Norman Brice is 26 and listed as an editor. His wife is Annabel and they have a son, James G. age 1.

On the 1880 census Norman is 36, Annabel is 35, James is 11 and Henry is 7. On the 1900 census of Covington, Kentucky Norman is 55, Anna B. is 54, Henry is 27 and there is a Lucie Brice age 27.

Brown, Emily Charlene   b 1851   d 4 Dec 1853   2 y 8 m 7 d

Emily was the daughter of James and Caroline Brown. I was not able to find much information on this family. On the 1850 census James and Caroline Irvin Brown are living in White River Township with Caroline's parents, Robert and Hannah Irvin.

Brown, Laura   b 2 Sep 1847   d 5 Sep 1847   3d

I was unable to find any information about this baby. The names of her parents are unknown and are not on her gravestone. Is she a sister to Emily (above)? This we may never know.

Brown, Sarah   b 1 Dec 1797   d 22 Dec 1871   74y 21d

On the 1860 census of White River Township, Thomas Brown is 68 and a farmer, Sarah is 62, Elizabeth is 30 and Martha is 22. Also living in the home is James Metz, listed as an orphan.

Death Notice, Winchester Journal, December 27, 1871:

"Mrs. Brown, an aged lady, wife of Thomas Brown of this city, died on Friday last of congestive chills. She was a most estimable lady."

Brown, Thomas   b 16 Nov 1792   d 20 May 1877   84 y 6m 14d

Thomas Brown was born in Lancaster County, Pennsylvania and was of Scottish descent. In 1831 he moved to Montgomery County, Ohio, then to Darke County, Ohio and then to Randolph County where he settled in the woods near Winchester. His wife, Sarah Rogers Brown was born in Philadelphia. Her father served in the Revolutiionary War for seven years. They were married in Ohio on May 14, 1817. They parented a total of eight children, the oldest five born in Ohio and the youngest three born in Winchester.

Obituary, Winchester Journal,

"Died at the residence of his son-in-law, Esquire Welker in Winchester, Thomas Brown on the 20th day of May 1877, aged 84 years, 6 months and 14 days. The deceased had been a citizen of this county for about 43 years. He was highly respected by all who knew him being a good neighbor, an affectionate husband and a kind father. His wife preceded him to the spirit land some five or six years ago. Age and bodily deformity had prevented him from mixing much with the active scenes of life for several years but he was patiently waiting and abiding his time. He had for many years been connected with the Christian Church and expressed in his last affliction great confidence and assurance that all was well, that death had no terror to him. He leaves three sons and two daughters to mourn the loss of their kind father. Two of his sons were not permitted to attend his funeral, his son, Thomas, being a citizen of Iowa and Rev. John Brown of U. B. Church of Huntington, Ind. His funeral services were conducted by Rev. John A. Moorman at the M.E. Church in Winchester."

Probate Court:

"State of Indiana, Randolph County, in the Randolph Circuit Court, February Term A. D. 1878. The matters of the estate of Thomas Brown deceased. John A. Moorman administrator of said estate show to said court that said decedent died intestate, that the personal assets of said estate amounted to about $346.42, that the debts of said estate so far as they have come to the petitioner's knowledge, amount to about $800.00, showing an insufficiency of the personal estate to pay debts of $453.58. That the decedent died the owner of the North half of the West half of Lot number seven in Frazee's Addition to the Town of Winchester in the County of Randolph and State of Indiana of the value of $60.00 and also of the West half of the North half of Lot number two in the South West Square of said town of Winchester, County and State aforementioned of the value of $600. That said decedent left no widow but left surviving him the following children and heirs at law to wit, James Brown, Thomas Brown, John Brown, Elizabeth Parker and Martha Welker and Sarah Addington and Nathan Addington (her husband)."

John Moorman went on to list the following assets and their values:

One Stove	$3.50	One lot of carpet	$1.00
One Bureau	1.00	One clock	.50
One Stand	.15	Lot of cooking utensils	.25
One blanket and two		Two chairs	1.25
pillows	.75	One bed and bedding	2.00
One feather bed	1.50		$11.90

Two of their daughters, Elizabeth Parker and her husband Melvin, and Martha Welker and her husband Squire, are buried in the Old Winchester Graveyard in a family plot with Thomas and Sarah. Their stories are written further along in the book.

Bunch, Infant   b ?   d 9 Sep 1860   ?

Infant daughter of L.D. and R.

Bunch, Rebecca   b 4 Nov 1823   d 6 Aug 1860   36 y 9m 2d

Obituary, Winchester Journal, August 9, 1860:

> "Died__In this place, very suddenly, on the evening of the 6th,
> Mrs. Rebecca Bunch, wife of L.D. Bunch. The funeral services
> were performed at the M.E. Church by the Rev. M.J. Hiatt, as-
> sisted by the Rev. L.A. Campbell of the Presbyterian church on
> the 7th. A large number of citizens, friends and relatives were
> present."

The infant daughter listed above died about one month after Rebecca.

I was not able to find L.D. Bunch on any census reports in Randolph
County so do not know if there were other children.

Bunch, Thomas   b 20 Jul 1832   d 23 Sep 1860   28 y 2 m 3 d

On the 1860 census of White River Township, Thomas Bunch is 28
and listed as a merchant, his wife, Jane, is 22 and they have Carie age
3 and Ida age 10 months.

Bunch, Unknown   stone unreadable

Daughter of ?

It is not known if the above people who share the same name are
related.

Bundy, Mary L.   b 1854   d 28 Aug 1854   1y 13d

On same gravestone marker as mother, Minerva

Bundy, Minerva E.   b 1833   d 29 Aug 1854   21y 5m 1d

Wife of B.F. Their baby daughter, Mary, died one day before Minerva. One could speculate that they had some sort of contagious infection. Deaths were more common in August than in any other month, largely due to the heat and humidity of Indiana which stimulated the occurrence of infectious diseases.

One source I will cite frequently is Portraits and Biographical Records, Randolph County, Indiana by A. W. Bowen. About B. F. Bundy he writes the following:

" Benjamin F. Bundy was born on the old homestead (of his father), near Centerville, Wayne County, March 7, 1828, and until sixteen years of age resided on the farm, attending such schools as the country afforded in the meantime. While still a youth, he learned the saddler's trade at Centerville, and worked as a journeyman for some time in several of the leading cities of the west and south, including St. Louis, Mo., Springfield, Ill., Memphis, Tenn. and New Orleans, La. In 1850 he opened a shop in the town of Huntsville, Ind., where he continued eight years, and about 1858, built a saw mill three miles southwest of Winchester and began the manufacture of lumber. He subsequently disposed of this mill, but afterwards repurchased it and at this time is operating it very properly. In 1877, Mr. Bundy embarked in the general mercantile trade in Winchester, previous to which date he had been associated in the same business with Robert Morrow, a firm which began operations about the year 1875. He continued the good business for eight years, disposing of his interests in Winchester at the end of that time, and resuming agricultural pursuits, having previously purchased a valuable farm in Section 6, White River Township. The farm contains 320 acres. Among the improvements is a large commodious barn, 60 x 120 feet in size, well arranged with a large basement under the entire building.

Mr. Bundy has been twice married; the first time to Miss Minerva Irvin, daughter of Robert Irvin, of Winchester, a union severed by death three years after its consummation. The second marriage was solemnized with Sarah J. Heaston, of Winchester, who died October 27, 1880. In addition to the vocations enumerated in which Mr. Bundy engaged, he was for some time identified with the profession of dentistry in partnership with A.J. Ross, under whose instruction he made substantial progress in the practice, and he also operated a photograph gallery for a limited period of time.

For a number of years Mr. Bundy was a local politician of the old Whig school, but on the disintegration of that party, became identified with its successor, the republican, with which he acted upon all questions of a state and national character until within a recent date. At this time he is practically independent in matters political, preferring to vote for the man best fitted to fill official position rather than adhere strictly to the creed of party."

Minerva and baby Mary could have had prosperous lives had they lived. And husband, Benjamin Franklin Bundy, certainly made the most of his American dream, working successfully in so many professions.

Burke, Quintilla   b 1852   d 7 Jun 1873   20 y 9 m

Until her marriage to Henry, Quintilla lived with her parents, Elijah A. Corbin and Phebe Urey Corbin and had the following siblings: Elizabeth, William, Elijah D., Isabel and Lewis H. She married Henry on October 2, 1869 in Randolph County in a ceremony performed by Jacob Eltzroth.

Obituary, Winchester Journal, June 11, 1873:

"Died__In this city, on Sunday morning last at 10 o'clock, Mrs. Quintilla Burke, aged 20 years and 9 months, wife of Henry Burke. The deceased was the daughter of Elijah A. Corbin and had been a resident of this place for several years past. She leaves a husband and one little boy to mourn her early death. Her disease is supposed to have been the Spinal Fever, the first case that has been in our town for some time."

Burris, Thomas   b 25 Jan 1835   d 16 Jun 1857   22y

I was not able to find any information about Thomas.

Burton, Edmund   b 1780   d 1865   80 y

Burton, Esther   b 1796   d 7 Oct 1861   65 y 9 m 2 d

On the 1850 census in White River, Edmund was 71 and a farmer and wife, Esther was 56. Both were listed as being born in England. They are listed with the following children: John age 7, a farmer, James age 16, Sarah age 15, Thomas age 11 and Margaret, age 20.

On the 1860 census in Winchester*, Edmund is 80, Esther is 65, Sarah is 25 and Thomas is 21.

*the dates on the census are a few years off, but clearly this is the same family

Campbell, Hester   b 1803   d 29 Nov 1860   76 y 8 m 8 d

Hester was married to John Campbell on October 16, 1839 in Jefferson County, Indiana. Her maiden name was Dickerson. I did not find any other information.

Canada, Clarence W.   b 1866   d 1869   3y

Clarence was the son of Wesley and Carrie E.

According to A.W. Bowen, in Portraits and Biographical Records, Randolph County, Indiana, found at the Randolph County Historical Society Museum, William W. was born in Stony Creek Township, Randolph County on June 8, 1850, the son of David and Mary A. Canada. He was one of ten children. After completing his education, William entered the law office of Moorman Way to continue his legal studies and went on to become a prominent lawyer in Winchester. He married Carrie E. Moore, daughter of James Moore, an early settler of Randolph County. In addition to Clarence W., they had children Lance and Coral.

Carter, Eliza E.   b 1843   d 5 Feb 1869   26 y 2 m 14 d

Eliza married Franklin B. Carter in Randolph County on June 21, 1855. Her maiden name was Ennis. On the 1860 census in Randolph County, Frank is 26, Elizabeth E. is 23 and they have a son, Henry age 4 months.

Carter, James E.   b 27 Apr 1856   d 20 May 1856   23 d

James was the son of F.B. and E.E. above.

CHAPTER SIX

HELLO, MY NAME IS JONNIE CARTER

I'm Jonnie Carter and I was born May 11, 1857. Really my name is John D. Carter, but Mommy and Daddy called me their "little Jonnie" and that's what everybody else called me too. My Daddy's name was Levi. He was born in Ohio. My grandparents moved to Randolph County in 1840. Daddy was a blacksmith and a wagon maker.

He married my Mommy in 1853. Her name was Hannah Hutchens. They had me first, then my sister, Lula and then my brother, Edmund.

My Aunt Nancy, who was my Daddy's sister, married Daniel Hoffman. He had the marble works here in Winchester and made most of the headstones you see here in our graveyard. They are almost all made of marble and hand carved. He carved a little boy lying down on the top of my gravestone. My Aunt Nancy and Uncle Daniel had five children, and three of them died too, but I don't know where they are buried. (They are at Fountain Park Cemetery) I wonder if Uncle Daniel made their gravestones. My aunt and uncle must have been very sad.

I don't know what made me die when I was five years old in December of 1862. Lots of children died. Sometimes Mommies died too. Mommy said that only about half of the children born lived until their fifth birthday. About a third of the burials in our graveyard are babies and young children.

Seemed like some friend or other child I knew was always dying. It was the worst in the summer, especially in August, because everyone caught diseases from each other. Some died from measles and scarlet fever and croup and whooping cough. I think the most died from diarrhea and vomiting.

There were lots of sad parents and grandparents. Some people didn't even name their babies at first, I guess thinking it wouldn't hurt as bad if they died if they were just called "baby" and not some name that made them more real, but I don't really think that helped.

It was a lot of fun to live in Winchester and play with all my friends. We could run all over town and everybody knew us and looked after us. Mostly we made our own toys out of sticks and stuff and played a lot of pretend games. On hot days we could get in the creek and cool off as long as someone older was with us. I didn't live long enough to get in on some of the great adventures the older children made up, but sometimes I watched them. I really liked horses and frogs.

My brother and sister got to live and grow up and have their own children. Mommy and Daddy moved to Muncie in 1888 and when they died they got buried there. I'm the only one from my family buried here, but I get lots of visitors. Sometimes people leave toys and sometimes flowers. I'm glad I am not forgotten.

Carter, John D.　　　b 1857　　　d 12 Dec 1862　　　5 y 7 m 18d

If you walk through the Old Winchester Graveyard, you will find the tombstone of Jonnie Carter, the five year old son of Levi D. and Hannah Carter. It stands out because there is a carving of a child lying on his side on top of the stone. It inspired former Winchester resident, I. Marlene King, to include his death as part of the plot in the movie she wrote, "Now and Then," about growing up in Winchester. The movie came out in 1998 and is still one of the most watched movies available on DVD. If you haven't seen it I would encourage you to do so.

Jonnie's gravesite is one of only seven left intact at the time the restoration of the graveyard was started. It is the best known of all the gravesites, and the most visited. I don't think that anyone could look at that sleeping child carved atop his gravestone and turn it over, or try to break it, or remove it. Even destructive people have their limits, and we are all grateful that Jonnie's stone was left intact and at its original burial site.

The most frequent question I get about the graveyard is "What caused our Jonnie to die?" Research has not given us the answer. However, an article published by the Chicago Public Library staff on 19th and 20th Century Infant and Childhood Mortality gives us some insight. In 1879 a newborn had only a 50% chance of living to the age of five, and the odds were even worse earlier in the 1800's. Whole families were subject to cholera, smallpox, measles and other bacterial and viral infections for which there was neither prevention nor treatment. Deaths were higher in the summer. A very common cause of death was dehydration caused from diarrhea. Accidental deaths were also common, frequently from fire and drowning.

For me, Jonnie Carter is representative of all the infants and children buried in the Old Winchester, most without a memorial stone. What sadness our ancestors had to endure.

Jonnie's parents were early residents of Winchester. From a biographical sketch in Tucker's History of Randolph County, 1882, we learn that Levi came to Randolph County in 1840 at age 16. In 1846 he worked as a blacksmith apprentice in Preble County, Ohio. After working at his trade for several years in various places, he returned to Winchester in 1851 and remained here. Besides blacksmithing he was engaged in the manufacture of wagons and carriages with one of his brothers. He was described as "enterprising and energetic, and by a life of industry has accumulated a comfortable fortune. In 1853 he married Hannah E Hutchens, an estimable lady who has been a devoted helpmate to him and a potent factor in his success." They had three children, two of whom, Lula and Edmund, reached adulthood.

Levi Carter's parents were Edmund D. and Mary (Diltz) Carter. They had nine children, two of whom died in childhood. All of the siblings prospered in Randolph County.

Descendents of this Carter family continue to live in the community. There is considerable information about the generations of Carters in Randolph County and in Winchester available in the Randolph County Historical Museum. They are a good example of the many families who came here and succeeded in our county and city.

CHAPTER SEVEN

CHAPMAN, WILLIAM- GINTHER, HENRY

Chapman, William D.   b 1863   d 16 Aug 1883   20y

William was found with his family on the 1870 Census living in Washington Township, Wayne County, Indiana. His father was Joseph, who was 34 and had a retail liquor business. His mother was Arabella and his sibling was Joseph age 10. William D. was five at the time of the census.

While the dates do not match exactly, the information on his tombstone says that he is the son of Joseph Chapman and Bell Dillihunt Chapman.

Churchman, F. Alexina   b 1853   d 5 Jul 1853   3 m 10 d

Her stone says that she is the daughter of G.A and Catherine. On the 1860 census, Ward Township, Randolph County, there is a George Churchman, age 39 who was a blacksmith. His wife was Catherine who was 34. They had two children, L.J., age 6 and Sarah, age 4 months. I did not find them on the 1870 census, but in 1880 they were residing in Redkey, Jay County, Indiana. G.A. was age 59 and a blacksmith, Catherine was age 54 and keeping house, and no children were listed.

Clark, Eliza Ann   b 1818   d 17 Mar 1859   41y ? m 21 d

A marriage license was issued on October 13, 1838, to Edward Clark and Eliza Ann Huston. On the 1850 census in Jefferson Township, Preble County, Ohio, Edward is 32 and a farmer, Eliza A. is 33. They have the following children: Henry, age 9, Mary R., age 8, Benjamin, age 6, Rachel, age 4 and James A., age 1. At some point before the 1860 census they must have moved to Randolph County and probably to Winchester since Eliza died in 1859, but I did not find any of them on other records.

Clevenger, Infant   b 6 Mar 1875   d 8 Mar 1875   2 d

She was the daughter of Stephen and Julie A. Clevenger.

Death Notice, Winchester Journal, March 10, 1875:

> "The little two day old babe of Stephen Clevenger died very suddenly last Monday evening. Cause unknown."

Clevenger, Julie A.   b 24 Nov 1846   d 7 June 1883   36 y 4 m14 d

On the 1880 census of White River Township, Stephen is 32 and a farmer, Julia is 33 and their two children are Carlos W. age 4 and Walter L. age 9 months. Three other children besides the infant above died before Julia and are buried in an unknown place, but probably the Old Winchester Graveyard.

Obituary, Winchester Journal, June 6, 1883:

> " Died__CLEVENGER__On the 7th inst. at home in Winchester, Julia A Clevenger, wife of Stephen Clevenger. The deceased was the daughter of Geo. O. Jobes, formerly of this city and now a resident of Indianapolis. She was born near Washington in Wayne County on the 24th of November 1846 and was consequently

aged thirty-six years, four months and fourteen days. In 1852 she, with her parents, removed to Huntsville in this county, and here the after years of her childhood were spent except for a short residence in this city. She received a fair education in common schools, and afterwards spent several years of her life teaching in them. She was married to Stephen Clevenger on the 18th day of September, 1873. In the few years of her married life she became the mother of five children, four of whom have already gone before to the better land. Her constitution, forever strong, was broken down. The burdens, cares and sorrows of subsequent years, told upon her with such fearful effect, that about 3 years ago she became insane, and her reason has been more or less clouded ever since. As child and woman she was loving, truthful and dutiful. She loved the right for its own sake, and with a conscience almost morbidly positive strove to do it in all the relations of life. Those who knew her in girlhood will never forget with what a tender self-sacrificing devotion she waited upon her invalid mother, lightening her burdens and anticipating her wants with a solicitude beyond her years. Her sterling qualities endeared her to the hearts of many who will sincerely sympathize with her husband and other relations in this their sad bereavement. She loved the Lord, and tried to keep His commandments, as she understood them, hoping for a happy reunion of the loved ones gone before. Hers was a Christianity without a creed or profession, but if it was true 'that a worthy life is the best passport to a happy eternity', she shall not therefore want for a crown."

Clevenger, Martha   b 19 Jul 1807   d 19 Feb 1875   67 y 7 m

Wife of Samuel Watts first, then Elias Clevenger, Martha was the mother of I.P. Watts.

Obituary, Winchester Journal, March 3, 1875:

" DIED at the residence of I. P. Watts, Friday night, Feb 19ᵗʰ at half past 11 o'clock P.M., MARTHA M. CLEVENGER, aged 67 years and seven months. The deceased was the daughter of Isaiah and Lydia Paxton. She was born on the 19ᵗʰ day of July, A.D. 1807, in Chester Co., Pennsylvania. In 1818 her father moved to Columbiana Co., Ohio and in 1828 or 29 he moved to Richland Co., Ohio, where she was married to Samuel Watts, Sept. 7, 1830; she was the mother of six children by him, two daughters and four sons, five of whom are still living. In 1846, Samuel Watts moved to Wells County Indiana, and they commenced anew in the woods, to make a farm and together, they endured the hardships of a pioneer life. Samuel Watts (her husband) died March 3ʳᵈ, 1859, and in Sept, 1864 she was married to Elias Clevenger, and lived with him up to the date of her death. In 1822, she became a member of the old Christian Church and in 1837 she united with the Disciples at Newville, Ohio, and has been a faithful member ever since. She was a zealous worker in the Master's cause and 'contended earnestly for the faith' and lived in constant hope of a blessed immortality.

She was a beloved wife, a tender hearted and loving mother and a sympathetic friend to those in trouble. The poor never turned away empty from her door, or failed to find a friend in need. 'She fought a good fight, she kept the faith' and has gone to that rest which remains for the people of God."

One of her son, I.P Watts, is mentioned frequently in Winchester history. He was a prominent lawyer in the community.

Colgrove, Harry Winfield   b 25 Jul 1879   d 19 Sep 1880   14m

Harry was the son of Theodore F. and Lotta and the grandson of Gen. Silas Colgrove.

Obituary, Winchester Journal, October 6, 1880:

"Little Harry Winfield, son of T.F. and Lotta Colgrove, aged 14 months, died suddenly of croup, last Wednesday evening. The parents have the sympathy of many friends in their sad bereavement. " Note in the paper the same day: "To all of those kind friends who manifested so much sympathy for us in our bereavement, we return our heartfelt thanks. Lotta and T.F. Colgrove."

Colgrove, Napoleon Bonaparte   b 1850   d 1866   16 y 7 m

Napoleon was the son of General Silas and Rebecca Colgrove. On the 1850 census of Winchester, Silas is 34 and an attorney, Rebecca is 30 and they have the following children: Bonaparte age 10, Washington age 7, Theodore age 6 and Silas W. age 1. On the 1860 census Silas is 44, Rebecca is 40, Washington is 17, Theodore is 16, Silas is 11, Olive is 9 and Charley is 7.

From Bowen's biographical book we learn the following:

"Gen. Silas Colgrove is a native of Steuben County, N.Y., and was born on the 24th of May, 1816. He is one of a family of eighteen children, of whom all but one grew to maturity and were married and fifteen are still living. Five reside in New York, three in Ohio and others in Indiana, Illinois, Minnesota and California. In 1837, Gen. Colgrove was united in marriage to Miss Rebecca P. Stone, in New York, and in the fall of the same year left home with his bride for the west. He began the study of law at his home in New York, completing his course of preparation in the office of Zachariah Puckett. He was admitted to the bar of Randolph County in 1839, and has been one of its foremost members in the years that have followed. In April 1839, he was elected justice of the peace, and served five years in that capacity. In 1852, he was elected prosecuting attorney for the district composed of the counties of Randolph, Henry, Wayne, Jay, Blackford, Grant and Delaware, in which capacity he served two years. In 1856 he was elected representative to the state legislature, serving two years and was re-elected. His term of office had scarcely expired when a call to arms was made. He was the first in this county to raise a company, and his own name was the first on the roll of enlisted men. It was enrolled as a private soldier, and he expected to serve in that capacity, but in three days he had a company of 140 men, and before they left for Indianapolis he was elected captain by a unanimous vote. Of this number, 100 were accepted for the three month's service. This company was assigned to the Eighth regiment, and Capt. Colgrove was commissioned lieutenant colonel. The regiment was in Maj. Gen. McClellan's army, in the West Virginia campaign, with Gen. Rosecrans as their brigade commander. They took part in the battle of Rich Mountain and assisted in the capture of Garnett's forces. At the expiration of his term of enlistment, Col. Colgrove returned to Winchester, and assisted in organizing the Eighth regiment for the three years of service. Shortly afterward, however, he was appointed colonel of the twenty-seventh regiment Indiana volunteers, which was placed under the command of Brig. Gen. Banks. They took part in the terrible battle at Ball's Bluff and helped to convey the dead across the Potomac after the fight. The regiment was a part of the army of the Potomac, serving first with the Fifth and afterward with the Eleventh corps, and participated in all of the important battles in which these corps were engaged. Finally, the eleventh and twelfth were consolidated under the name of the Twentieth army corps, with Gen Hooker in command, and sent to Chattanooga, where they joined Gen. Sherman, remaining with his army until the fall of Atlanta. During this period of service Col. Colgrove was wounded several times, but remained bravely at his post, although his injuries were sufficiently serious to justify him leaving the service, had he chosen to do so. His distinguished services were recognized by President Lincoln, who conferred upon him the rank of brigadier general, by brevet, on the 7th day of August, 1864. He resigned later in that year, and returned to his home in Winchester, having, in the meantime, been appointed by Gov. Morton to fill the unexpired term of Judge Elliott, who had been chosen one of the judges of the supreme court of Indiana. In the same year he was elected president of the Cinncinnati, Fort Wayne &Grand Rapids railroad, and on the 19th of December, 1864, he was appointed president of the military commission for the trial of Horsey, Milligan and Bowles, the traitors. The trial was in progress for a period of 100 days, and the defendants were found guilty and sentenced to death. This sentence, however, was commuted to imprisonment for life, and the trio were finally set free by the supreme court of the United States, on the ground that a military tribunal has no jurisdiction over the offense. In 1865, Gen. Colgrove was elected judge of the circuit court, composed of Randolph, Wayne, Henry, Jay, Blackford and Grant Counties, serving six years. In 1873 he was again elected to this office, continuing to occupy the bench until 1879. Retiring from this position he resumed the practice of his profession. As an attorney, he has attained marked success, as a judge his opinions were always profound and his decisions just. As a citizen, he has always been enterprising and public spirited, and during his residence in this county he has been identified with many of its public improvements. In politics he affiliated with the whig party during its existence, but afterward became a Republican, and has ever since continued to act with that party. He united with the Odd Fellows at Winchester at an early day. He has lived nearly half a century in this community, and by an upright, honorable life has gained the confidence and esteem of all who know him. His wife, Miss Rebecca P. Stone, was born in Steuben County, N.Y, March 30, 1820 and died in August, 1887.

> To bless their wedded life, there were eleven children, four of whom are now living. One son became celebrated as an aeronant, but lost his life in the pursuit of his perilous profession, near San Francisco, Cal."

In Rebecca's obituary she was described as someone " notable not only for her extremely kind and neighborly acts, but more especially for her unswerving and devoted loyalty to her country and its service, gladly and proudly giving up at the first call her husband the only two sons old enough to go, and ever since being the devoted friend of all who were identified with or friendly to the cause." Rebecca had a fall and broke a hip in January of 1886. She also had cancer and after a three year battle she died August 9, 1887. She is buried in Fountain Park. General Colgrove died at the age of 90, residing at the home of a granddaughter in Florida.

Even though it is the son and grandsons of General and Mrs. Colgrove who are buried in the Old Winchester, this family has contributed much to the history of Winchester and their story deserves to be told. There is also considerable information available on ancestry.com.

Colgrove, Wilford H.   b 1874   d 25 Jun 1875   10 m 17 d

Wilford was the son of Washington Lafayette and Hattie Pinkerton Colgrove and the grandson of Gen. Silas and Rebecca Colgrove.

Obituary, Winchester Journal, June 30, 1875:

> "Died__At Indianapolis on Friday last, after a short illness from Spinal Fever, WILFORD H., son of W.L. and Hattie Colgrove, aged 10 months and 17 days. Funeral services were held at Friend's Church last Saturday afternoon by Rev. Henry A. Merrill.

Mrs. C. was visiting her mother and other relatives at Indianapolis at the time her babe was taken sick. The parents have the sympathy of many friends in the hours of their trial."

On the 1880 census of Winchester, W.L. was 37 and a deputy sheriff, H.L. was 36, and their two children were Shields C., age 10 and G. B., age 7.

Condon, Patrick   b 1843-44d ?   d ?   ? y

Enlisted 11 Oct 1861 at age 18 in Co. H, 68th Infantry Regiment, Ohio and mustered out Company H, 68th Infantry Regiment on 10 Jul 1865 at Louisville, Kentucky

When gravestones were found broken and buried, Patrick's military marker was found and restored. No information could be found about him including when he came to Winchester and why, when he died or even any record of him in Ohio except for his military enlistment. There is also a discrepancy in his military regiment. Information from the military records lists him in the 68th Infantry, and his gravestone lists him in the 60th Infantry Regiment. A new military marker has since been placed in his memory.

Conner, Charles Theodore   b 1858   d 14 Sep 1860   2 y 9 d

Death Notice, Winchester Journal, September 16, 1860:

"DIED__On the 14th inst., Charles Theodore Conner, son of William and Catherine P. Conner, aged 2 years and 9 days."

Conner, Caroline E.   b 1841   d 3 Aug 1861   20 y 1 m 5 d

Winchester Journal, May 19, 1859:

"Married: On 6th inst., by Jacob Eltzroth, Esq., Mr. Jesse Conner to Miss Caroline Way, both of Winchester. We have been of the opinion for a long time that Cal. would finally catch JESSE, and so it has turned out. Well, we give our consent and would not object if they should conclude to marry again in a few days, if a cake so magnificent should again fall to our lot. We hope that Jesse may ever be found faithful to the WAY he had chosen."

On the 1860 census of White River Township, Jesse is 24 and a day laborer, Caroline E. is 19 and they have a baby, Loretta B. age 7 months.

Caroline is the second wife of Jesse and the daughter of Jesse Way and Lucinda Turner Way.

I found a marriage certificate for Jesse Conner and Mariah Hutchens in Randolph County for September, 1853. Jesse would have been 17 when they married. I did not find any information about Mariah, nor did we find a tombstone for her. Mariah would have been Jesse's first wife.

Conner, Lavina N.   b 1845   d 23 May 1868   23 y 10 m 14 d

Lavina is Jesse's third wife. They were married January 13, 1867 in Wayne County, Indiana.

Caroline and Lavina are buried next to each other and have identical markers.

On the 1870 census Jesse is listed as a huckster, age 34 with his fourth wife, Mary Conner. There are no children listed. I don't know what happened to Loretta B., his child with Caroline. On the 1900 census Jesse is 64, Mary is 50 and the census says they married in 1870. There is a George L. Conner age 22 living with them, perhaps a son.

Cottom, David J.   b 1846   d ?   ?

On the 1850 census of Winchester John W. Cottom is 32 and a merchant, his wife Eliza A. is 32 and their children are Evan J., age 9, David J,. age 4, Charles E., age 5 and Mary E., age 1.

The following biographical information is found in Bowen's book cited several times earlier:

"John W. Cottom, prominent in the insurance business at Winchester and formerly merchant on an extensive scale, was the first white child born at New Paris, Preble County, Ohio. His parents were John H. and Rebecca Jameson Cottom. John H. was born in Snow Hill, Md., June 4, 1788, and when ten years old was taken to Kentucky and was married in that state, located in New Paris, Ohio in 1812, and there the birth of John W. took place March 20, 1818. John H. Cottom conducted a general store in New Paris until 1829, when he went into the hotel business, which he conducted until 1838, when he retired. His death took place in Cincinnati in 1875, at the age of eighty-seven years. Mrs. Rebecca Jameson Cottom was born in Bourbon county, Ky., October 22, 1787, and passed away in 1864 at the age of seventy-seven years. They were the parents of four children named as follows: David J., deceased; Thomas F., deceased; John W., now of Winchester, and James S., deceased. Both parents were members of the Methodist Episcopal church and in politics the father was first a whig and later a republican.

John W. Cottom was reared in New Paris, Ohio, and remained there with his father until about 1845, when he came to Winchester and engaged in mercantile trade until 1857, when he went to Peoria, Ill., and carried on a wholesale tobacco business for two years; his next venture was at Cincinnati, Ohio, where for two years he was engaged in the wholesale dry goods trade; next he went into the wholesale boot and shoe business, which occupied his attention for four years; again resuming the wholesale dry goods business, he continued in that trade for ten long years, and then went to Douglas County Kansas, where he followed agriculture for seven years.

In 1884 he returned to Winchester and established an insurance agency, and in 1889 attached the loan business, in company with Wesley O. Smith under the name of Cottom & Smith, and is now doing a prosperous business. Mr. Cottom was married in his native town, June 18, 1839, to Miss Eliza A. Jones, a native of Chester County, Pennsylvania, born July 17, 1818, a daughter of Jacob and Phebe Cannon Jones, of Irish extraction. This union has been blessed with five children." The biography goes on to say he was a man of integrity. John W. lived to be 99 years old, dying in 1917. Eliza died in 1888. Both are buried in Fountain Park Cemetery."

Cottom, Louisa Caroline   b 1854   d 22 Aug 1855   9 m 22 d

Cottom, William Sherman   b 1865   d 1 Nov 1866   18 m

Louisa and William are the children of Samuel P. and Louisa J. On the 1860 census Samuel is 35 and a printer, his wife Louisa is 32 and their children are Belle age 5 and Henry age 2.

Cottom, Nancy   b 1796   d 3 Apr 1867   71 y

Obituary, Winchester Journal, April 11, 1867:

"COTTOM__In Winchester, on Wednesday, April 3rd, of consumption, after a long though patient suffering, Mrs. Nancy Cottom, wife of Mr. Thomas Cottom and mother of S.P Cottom, at the advanced age of 71 years. She died as she had lived, a faithful, consistent Christian, respected and beloved by all who knew her. 'Blessed are the dead which die in the Lord from henceforth; Yes sayeth the Spirit, that they may rest from their labors and their works do follow them.'"

Craig, Susannah   b 16 Aug 1794   d 3 Jun 1864   69 y 18 d

On the 1850 census of Washington Township, Randolph County, James Craig is 73 and a farmer, his wife, Susannah is 56 and their children are Thomas Craig age 19, John age 16 and Edgar age 13. Susannah had been married previously and her daughter, Elizabeth A. Dormer, age 33 was living with them. On the 1860 census of White River township, Randolph County, Susannah is head of household age 65, living with Eliza A., 44, Edgar, age 23 and William, age 28.

Susannah's will was recorded on June 18, 1864, as follows:

"Daughter, Eliza Ann Jane Dormer, all the estate, real and personal.... To children of James Dormer $1.00; to son Richard Dormer $1.00, to son James Dormer $1.00; to son Richard Dormer $1.00; to son Robert Dormer $1.00; to son William Craig $1.00; to son Thomas Craig $1.00; to son John Craig $1.00; to son Edgar Craig $1.00 and carpenter tools."

Demint, Brown   b 25 Jul 1852   d 13 Nov 1853   1 y 4 m

Brown was the son of John G. and Margaret Demint. On the 1850 census John is 37, Margaret is 35 and they have the following children: James age 11, Preston age 3 and Sarah A. age 1.

On the 1860 census John is 47 and a farmer, Margaret is 45 and their children are: James, age 21, Preston, age 13, Sarah, age 11, John S., age 5 and Jesse, age 2.

Many family members are buried at Riverside Cemetery in Ridgeville, Randolph County. Brown is also listed on a memorial marker, but his remains probably remain in the Old Winchester Graveyard. There is discrepancy on the dates on the two markers.

Dwyre, Mary   b Apr 1855   d 22 May 1855   1 m

On the tombstone it reads that Mary was the daughter of J. and M. On the 1860 census of Farmland, Indiana I found a John Dwire, age 36 and a day laborer, his wife Mary age 40 and the following children: Alice, age 10, Bridget, age 6, Catharine, age 15, Joanah, age 9, John, age 12 and Mary, age 3.

It is uncertain if the family on the census listed above are the family members of Mary Dwyre, but the evidence is strongly in favor of it. A gravestone was found with her name and birth and death dates. There were no other Dwyres or Dwires found on the census for Randolph County. The parents, John and Mary were born in Ireland. The children were born in N.Y., Ohio and the youngest, Mary, age 3, in Indiana. Mary would have been born two years after Mary Dwyre died. It was not unusual to give a baby the same name as a deceased sibling.

Dye, Mr.   d ? Jun 1838   ?

Newspaper article, Winchester Journal, Sept. 22, 1875:

"A stroll through the cemetery adjoining town reveals the sad fact that many of the graves are without monumental inscriptions by which a passerby may be informed who sleeps beneath the long neglected mound. Nearly one-half the graves are in this condition. The date of the oldest inscription was that of a Mr. Dye who died in June, 1836, yet it is certainly known that interments were made here prior to that date. At present there are several fine and costly monuments which make an imposing appearance. As we scanned the epitaphs inscribed upon them, the thought involuntarily occurred to us, did the lives and characters of those thus honored leave in the hearts of their neighbors' equally imposing monuments? But here is a grave of recent date, that of Mr. McLeaf, a wheel barrow or two of earth scooped out of it to repair a nearby grave. Here we also notice a new grave, arranged and decorated with many flowers tastefully arranged, at the head of which stands a neat and finely finished marble on which rests a lamb__a fit emblem of purity and innocence and a most appropriate monument erected in the memory of little Laura Heiks, who though dead still lives in the affections of all who knew her. These grounds for several years were allowed to be overgrown with brambles, but recently Mr. J. Heiks, with his own hands, grabbed and cleared the grounds which now present a greatly improved appearance."

From this microfilm newspaper article, I learned the names of three people buried there whose monuments we did not find. It also validated the belief that while the graveyard officially opened in 1844, burials were taking place for several years prior. Some remains may have been moved from the first Winchester burial grounds, the Conway cemetery to what became the Heaston Cemetery.

I did not, however, find any information about Mr. Dye.

Edwards, Elizabeth   b 1788   d 26 Dec 1863   75 y 3 m 3 d

On the 1850 White River Township census Jonathan Edwards is 60 and a farmer, his wife Elizabeth is 60 and living with them is son Levi age 20. On the 1860 census Jonathan is 70 and Elizabeth is 70.

No other information was found. Elizabeth has memorial markers in both the Old Winchester and the Fountain Park cemeteries, so it is uncertain where her remains are actually buried.

Edwins, Stanley Walter   b 2 Sep 1862   d 11 Aug 1863   11 m 9 d

On his gravestone it says he was the only child of S.W. and M.K. I was unable to match Stanley's parent's initials with any census in Randolph County. I did find his father's military record which stated he was a resident of Winchester, Indiana who enlisted September 28, 1864 as an asst. surgeon during the Civil War. He was commissioned an officer on October 18, 1864 and mustered out on 31 Aug, 1865 in Greensboro, N.C. Baby Stanley W.'s father was also named Stanley W. On the 1870 census I found Stanley W. Edwins, age 34 and a physician in Monroe Township, Putnam County, Indiana, living with wife Mary age 30 and adopted son, Theodore, age 3. In 1880, they were living in Pipe Creek Township, Madison County, Indiana. Stanley was 44and Mary K. was 38. Theodore was listed as adopted son, age 13 and also listed was Flora May Edwins, age 6.

I don't know when Mary K. died, but Stanley's father's story did not have a happy ending. In the Directory of Deceased American Physicians, 1804-1929, on ancestry.com, it lists Stanley W. Edwins as dying on 16 Nov 1918 at the age of 82 of suicide by gunshot.

Through researching findagrave.com, I learned that he was buried in Elwood, Madison County, Indiana. His obituary from the Elwood Call-Leader, 18 Nov 1918 reads as follows:

> " Masonic Honors for Dr. Edwins: The funeral of Dr. S.W. Edwins was conducted at his late residence this afternoon at 2 o'clock by Rev. C.J Bunnell of Rushville, former pastor of the Elwood Baptist Church. The Masonic fraternity, of which Dr. Edwins was a devoted member, conducted their funeral services at the

residence. The Grand Army of the Republic post escorted the body to the city cemetery and the officers gave the ritual of the order at the mausoleum, where the body was placed in its last resting place beside the members of his family. (author note, no survivors were mentioned in his obituary)

Verdict of the Coroner: Earl Sells came from Anderson Saturday afternoon and held a brief examination of the circumstances of the death. He gave a verdict of death by suicide, a bullet wound from a revolver having been intentionally inflicted. In the passing of Dr. Edwins, Elwood loses one of its oldest residents and an unusual character. He was a man strong in likes and dislikes."

Eltzroth, Elizabeth (Neff)   b 16 Oct 1796   d 20 Sep 1864   68 y

Marriage Dec. 11, 1817 in Preble County, Ohio, Jacob Eltzroth (son of Nicholas Eltzroth and Susan Shock) and Mary Elizabeth Neff (daughter of John Neff and Susan Gray)

On the 1850 census of Winchester Jacob is 53, Elizabeth is 51, Emaline is 23, James M. is 17, Lewis C. is 5 and Warren R. is 2. On the 1860 census Jacob is 63, Elizabeth is 63, John N. is 42, Warren is 13 and Rolly W. is 11.

Eltzroth, Jacob   b 1794   d 20 Mar 1871   76 y

Obituary, Winchester Journal, April 5, 1871:

"ANOTHER PIONEER GONE: DIED, in this city, on Wednesday, March 20th, 1871, Jacob Eltzroth, in his 77th year. The subject of this notice was so well known to a large majority of our residents, that any extended notice would seem superfluous; and we shall indulge in none, save to add a tribute of respect to the good man who was so suddenly called from our midst. When we penned those few lines for our last issue-"Squire Eltzroth was attacked with a sinking chill this morning", we little thought it would be our mournful duty to chronicle his demise in so short a time, hoping that his naturally strong constitution would withstand the shock, and that he would again revive; and yet ere our article had reached our readers' eyes, we were startled with the word that "Uncle Jakey" as he was familiarly known, had passed from among us and gone to the spirit land.

"ANOTHER PIONEER GONE: DIED, in this city, on Wednesday, March 20th, 1871, Jacob Eltzroth, in his 77th year. The subject of this notice was so well known to a large majority of our residents, that any extended notice would seem superfluous; and we shall indulge in none, save to add a tribute of respect to the good man who was so suddenly called from our midst. When we penned those few lines for our last issue-"Squire Eltzroth was attacked with a sinking chill this morning", we little thought it would be our mournful duty to chronicle his demise in so short a time, hoping that his naturally strong constitution would withstand the shock, and that he would again revive; and yet ere our article had reached our readers' eyes, we were startled with the word that "Uncle Jakey" as he was familiarly known, had passed from among us and gone to the spirit land.

'Squire Eltzroth was born in Potatot County, Virginia in 1794. Of his early years we have not been able to gather the particulars beyond the fact that he removed to or near Eaton, Ohio at an early age, from whence he removed to Winchester in 1832 where he resided until his death. He was elected Justice of the Peace for this township in 1837, and with the exception of an interval of one year has held that honorable position ever since, over a third of a century. He was not only probably the oldest Justice in

Eastern Indiana, but was one of the oldest masons, having been initiated as a member of that fraternity in the Eaton Lodge in 1825, forty-seven years before his death. He was buried with the honors of the order, in our cemetery, on Friday last, the Deerfield and Farmland Lodges and large delegations from the Lynn and Huntsville Lodges, joining the Winchester Lodge in paying this last tribute to their departed brother. The procession that followed his remains was one of the largest, if not the largest, funeral procession ever seen in Winchester.

'Squire Eltzroth was emphatically that "noblest work of God"- an honored man. He had his foibles, and who has not? He was strong in his convictions of right and wrong, firm in his belief of duty, faithful to his friends. That his constituents had faith in his integrity is more eloquently expressed by repeated re-elections to his position, than by naught we could say. He was in many respects a peculiarly fortunate man. He had lived far beyond the time usually allotted to man- had reached a great old age without much physical suffering. During his life he never had but one spell of sickness that confined him to his room for any considerable length of time. His final sickness was of short duration, and he, happily, unconscious of suffering.

He had raised a large family and seen them comfortably started in the world. He had not accumulated a large amount of property, but left a sufficiency to support his bereaved wife in her declining years. His sudden death is another warning of the uncertainty of life and the certainty of death. May we all be as ready to meet the dreaded summons, when it comes, as we believe the deceased to have been."

Jacob had married his second wife, Maria Larrison, in Randolph County December 1, 1865, when he was 71 years of age.

Two of the sons of Jacob and Elizabeth died at a time when they would probably have been buried in the old cemetery. James M. died March 4, 1859 at the age of 25 y and Lewis C. died February 23, 1854 at the age of 19. Because we could not find any tombstones or record placing them in the graveyard, they are not on the list.

Ennis, Emma Lee   b 1862   d 31 Aug 1863   1 y 5 m 11 d

Ennis, Georgie W.   b 1864   d 20 Nov 1865   1 y 2 m 24 d

Emma and Georgie are the children of William and Rachael Ennis.

Marriage certificate, Randolph County, September 29, 1856, William W. Ennis and Rachel Remel.

On the 1850 census of Stony Creek Township, Randolph County, Lewis Remel is 38 and married to Mary, age 35. They have three daughters, Rachel, age 10, Semantha, age 7 and Mary A., age 5. On the 1860 census of White River Township, Randolph County, William Ennis is 23 and a day laborer, his wife Rachael is listed as age 20. Also living with them are Semantha Remel, age 17 and Mary Remel, age 15. There are no children listed for William and Rachel.

Ennis, Isabella Page   b 1814   d 1865   51 y

Isabella was the wife of James C. Ennis and the sister of William Page. James and Isabella were married in Randolph County on February 11, 1830.

On the 1850 census in Winchester, James is listed as 39 and a grocery keeper, Isabella is 38, Eliza E. is 14, Louisa E. is 11, Catharine is 7, William W. is 5 and Mary E. is 2.

On the 1860 census in Winchester, James C. Ennis is 49, Isabel is 48, Catherine W. is 17, William W. is 15 and Mary E. is 12.

In the Tucker History of Randolph County, 1882, James was listed as a member of the Winchester Methodist church in 1856 and in 1860 he is listed as an assessor and marshal.

Evans, B.W.   b 1815   d 12 Apr 1886   71 y 1 m 12 d

On the 1860 census, Green Township, Randolph County, B.W. Evans is 45 and is a thesician. (an occupation for the reader to research) His wife is Rebecca, age 33, and they are listed with the following children: Z.F., age 11, Ada Z., age 8, Sigasamer I,. age 6, Aaron L., age 2. The only other information I found that may fit with this person was in Tucker's History of Randolph County, 1882. Benjamin W. Evans is listed as being in Co.G.,124th Indiana and mustered out Aug 31, 1865 as a hospital steward. Because we could not be absolutely sure that this is the same person, we did not order him a military monument from the Civil War. He may deserve one.

Evans, Mary E.   b 1841   d 24 May, 1879   38 y 10 m 26 d

Obituary, Winchester Journal, May 28, 1879:

"DIED__On Saturday last, May 24, Mrs. MARY E. EVANS, wife of Dr. J.J. Evans, aged 38 years, 10 months and 27 days, of congestive fever. The deceased was born in Fairfield County, Ohio, and was married to Dr. Evans in May, 1860. She joined the German Reformed Church and was a faithful and consistent member until death. Death came upon her suddenly but found her ready. Funeral services were held at the residence Sabbath evening, by Rev. W.O. Pierce, after which the remains were interred in the Winchester cemetery.

Thus has passed away a wife and mother from our midst. The deceased was quiet and retiring in her disposition. Home was her throne and the domestic altar her crown. And this is the brightest ornament that can adorn the human heart, a meek and quiet spirit. In this day of bluster and parade, when there is such a clamoring for publicity, the spirit that is satisfied to excel is more than Queen or potentate. Such was the character of the deceased. More than this, she had the Christian's faith and this sustained her to the end. A bereaved husband, three motherless girls, an aged mother and three brothers are left to mourn. A FRIEND"

Evans, Tommy W.   b 1877   d 11 Aug 1877   9 m 13 d

Obituary, Winchester Journal, August 15, 1877:

"Died of diphtheria, Tommy W. Evans, only son of Dr. J.J. and Mary E. Evans on Saturday, August 11, 1877, aged 9 months and 13 days; whose death is mourned by relatives and friends."

The following poem was printed at the end of the obituary.

IN MEMORY OF THE BOY

The sweetest flowers that bloom in spring,
The soonest fade and die-
And scattered on each silent bed,
Their withered leaflets lie;
And every leaf though brown and scarred,
The pleasing thought doth bring,
That they will be more beautiful
When comes another spring.
Then we who only watch with eyes,
That often wake to weep
Over some friend or kindred dear,
When calm they fall asleep,

Should think that death is but the gate
That leads to endless joy;
And in a brighter, fairer clime,
Now lives their angel boy.
Too pure to dwell in this cold world,
Where grief alone hath place,
Some smiling seraph fondly gazed,
On his angelic face.
And bearing on its brilliant wing,
Back to his native sky,
Thy cherub-babe there sweetly lives,
to draw thy soul on high.
Tis sad, indeed, to part with those
We dearly love on earth;
But in a purer, brighter world
Their souls alone have birth;
So few the fleeting joys of time
To count their longer stay,
I mourn not when thus the young
And lovely pass away.
Friend, thy God has often been
The humble stranger's friend
Who dares with thy heart-rending grief
His sympathies to blend,
And he will fondly hope that when
Life's toilsome journey's o'er,
To dwell with those stricken ones,
Where sorrow comes no more.

On the 1880 census in Winchester Joseph J. Evans is listed as age 40, a widower, and a physician. Listed in the household with him are Alma, age 18, Minnie, age 17, Ettie, age 15 and Bell, age 13.

On the 1900 census Dr. J.J. is living in White River Township and has a second wife, Ellen M. age 45. Listed in the household is Ettie age 35 and Dale, age 13. By the 1910 census Dr. J. J. is widowed for the second time and is living with Rosetta (Etta) age 45. He died in 1918 and is buried in Fountain Park.

Both Mary and Tommy W. have restored gravestones in the Old Winchester and are therefore on the list of burials. However, they are also listed as being in Fountain Park. It is uncertain where their remains are actually buried, so they are maintained on both lists.

Everetts, Arlie Owens   b 1876   d 21 Mar 1877   1 y 4 m 1 d

Death Notice, Winchester Journal, March 28, 1877:

"DIED__In Winchester March 21st, 1877, infant son of A. and Sarah Everetts, aged 1 yr. 4 mos. and 1 day."

I was unable to find any information about this family.

Farra, Nancy   b 1821   d 28 Sep 1852   31 y 3 m 27 d

On the 1850 census of Winchester, John Farra is 28 and a hatter, his wife Nancy is 30 and they have two children, William A. age 8 and Phebe A. age 8 months. I did not find them on the 1860 census and on the 1870 census of Winchester John Farra is age 58, a hatter and is listed as a widower. He is living alone.

I found marriage records for John Farra in Randolph County in November, 1853, to Mary Jane Hubbard by M.S. H. Lucas and to Catherine Edwards on August 19, 1866, by Judge Silas Colgrove.

There is an error in John's age, probably on the 1870 census. I was unable to find any other information about this family. Only Phebe was born in Indiana. I do wonder what happened to William and Phebe after their mother's death.

Felt, Ella Mae   b 1880   d 2 May 1880   5 m 17d

On the 1880 census of White River Township, Freeman E. Felt is 32, Melinda is 27 and they have one child, Charles O. age 2. Also living with them is Hannah Felt, Freeman's mother age 62.

Death Notice, Winchester Journal, May 5, 1880:

> "DIED__Ella May, daughter of F.E. and Melinda Felt, on May 2, 1880, aged 5 months and 17 days. Funeral services were held at the family residence on Monday the 3rd at 3 o'clock p.m. conducted by Rev. R.D. Spellman."

Fie, Catherine (also spelled Fry)   b 1787   d 14 Sep 1867   80 y

Catherine came here from Germany. She is the mother of Philippine Harrman who is also buried in the Old Winchester Graveyard. There is more information about the family under the name Harrman.

Fitzpatrick, J. Harvey   b 4 Sep 1818   d 25 Mar 1873   54y

James Harvey was the son of William Fitzpatrick and Catherine Hawke.

On the 1850 census of Fairview, Randolph County, J.H. is 32 and a merchant, Elizabeth is 33 and their children are Jennett, age 4, Adaline, age 2 and William, age 2 months.

On the 1870 census in Winchester, Harvey is 52, a farmer, Elizabeth is 52, Ada is 21 and William is 19.

Obituary, Winchester Journal:

"Died at his residence in Winchester, Randolph Co., Ind., on the 25th of March 1873 of Catarrhal Fever and Ersipelas, J. HARVEY FITZPATRICK, aged 54 years. The deceased was born in Eaton, Preble Co., Ohio Sept. 4, 1818, and married Elizabeth in 1845. In the same year they moved to Camden, Jay Co., this State and removed to this county in 1847. He, like all the primitive settlers, bore the hardships of a new country and the sacrifices necessary to build it up.

Many of our old settlers can testify to his liberality toward churches, turnpikes and all enterprises which tend to the advancement, growth and general prosperity of a country. Many soldiers will remember with gratefulness with what generous heart his hand sought his purse to relieve their wants. Many testimonials of his virtue have come from absent friends to the bereaved family. One who had known him intimately said 'His family and friends will long remember him. His family as a kind husband and father, his friends as a generous, upright honest man, one who was trusted among his neighbors and known to be just in all the business relations of life.' He leaves a wife, two daughters and a son to mourn his loss."

Ford, Martha   b 1815   d 16 Feb 1863   47 y 3 m 14 d

On the 1850 census of Liberty Township, Fairfield County, Ohio, John W. Ford is 35 and a farmer, Martha is 34 and their children are Albert, age 8, Emaline, age 7, Sempta, age 5 and Enoch, age 2.

On the 1860 census of Ward Township, Randolph County, John W. is 47, Martha is 45, A.P. is 18, Emaline is 16, S is 14, Enoch W. is 12, Lucinda A. is 7 and Maranda J. is 5.

Fox, Maria   b 1847   d 24 Jul 1877   29 y 9 m

On the 1870 census of Winchester, Samuel Fox is 27 and listed as working in the tile factory, and Maria is 22 keeping house. No children are listed.

Obituary, Winchester Journal, July 25, 1877:

> "DIED__In this city at 5 o'clock yesterday morning, July 24 Mrs. Maria A. Fox, wife of Samuel D. Fox, aged 29 years and 9 months

> of Congestion of the Brain. The funeral services will be held at the M.E. church at 2 o'clock this afternoon conducted by Rev. B.A. Kemp. The deceased was the daughter of James Flemming and had lived here for many years. She was a most estimable lady, and leaves a husband, parents and many friends to mourn her sudden departure."

Frazier, Thomas   b 1836   1 Aug 1869   33 y 3 m 27 d

I was not able to find any information on Thomas.

Fulghum, J. Albert   b 1839   d 26 Aug 1870   31 y 6 m 27 d

A family tree on ancestry.com lists him as James Albert Fulghum born 1839 in Randolph County, a son of Joseph Fulghum and Rebecca T. Jessup.

Obituary, Winchester Journal, August 31, 1870:

"The funeral of Albert Fulghum last Sabbath was largely attended. He was buried with Masonic honors, Union City Lodge, of which he was a member, came over on a special train. The deceased was an engineer on the P.C.& St. L. R.R, and died suddenly at Logansport on Friday last, with congestive chills. He leaves a wife and several small children."

Gerstner, George G.   b 1809   d 5 Apr 1879   70 y

Marriage: George Gerstner married Charlotte Greenawalt on Oct. 26, 1852 in Darke County, Ohio by Paulis Herd, a Lutheran minister. Both were born in Germany.

On the 1860 census of White River Township, Randolph County, George is 52, Charlotte is 41 and their children, all born in Indiana, are Louisa, age 7, Charles, age 5 and Henry, age 2.

On the 1870 census in Winchester, George is 61 and a brewer, Louisa is 17, Henry is 12 and Minnie is 8.

Winchester Journal, April 23, 1879

"Administrator's Sale, Notice is HEREBY GIVEN, that the undersigned, Administrator of the Estate of George Gerstner, deceased, will sell at Public Auction, at the late residence of said deceased, in Winchester, Randolph County, Indiana, on Saturday, May 10, 1879, the following personal property, to wit: Beds and bedding, Bedsteads, Spring Mattress or Lounge, Bureau, Chairs, Tables, Carpets, Cupboard ware, Stoves, Sausage grinder and stuffer, Kettle, Corn, seventy-two beer kegs & c. Sale to begin at 10 o'clock a.m. Terms.-Sums of $3 and under, Cash; over $3 a credit of six months note with approved security with six percent interest from date, and waiving relief from valuation and appraisement laws. April 9, 1879, Asa Teal, Administrator, J.D. Carter, Auctioneer."

Winchester Journal, April 23, 1879

"George G. Keller was on Wed. last appointed Guardian of Minnie Gerstner. Bond $1,300."

Gerstner, Charlotte Greenawalt b 24 Aug 1811 d 25 Feb 1867 56 y

Charlotte was the daughter of Charles and Charlotte Greenawalt, who on the 1850 census lived in Greenville, Darke County, Ohio. Also on the census was Henry, age 19 and Louisa, age 7, siblings of Charlotte.

Gerstner, Charles   b 1854   d 1 June 1870   16 y

Article, Winchester Journal, June 9, 1870:

"SAD ACCIDENT, A BOY KILLED. It is our painful duty at the threshold of our Journalistic career at this place, to record one of the most shocking and terrible accidents that ever occurred in our prosperous town, to chronicle a fearful accident that resulted in the death of a fellow being in the hey-day of his youth, a sudden rending of soul and body whilst in perfect physical health. One of those occurrences that so shocks humanity, because of their suddenness and the manner of which the body of the unfortunate victim was mutilated.

The circumstances attending the casualty, as we learn them from eyewitnesses, are as follows: On Monday morning last the local freight, or as it is more popularly known, the accommodation train, had attached to it some passenger coaches intended for the use of the excursionists next day. After discharging their freight at the depot, the train moved up to the west side-track, cut the train in two, ran the coaches intended for this place on the siding, and were backing down for the purpose of getting the part of the train cut off. Before this, however, and while the train was standing, a son of Andy Aker got on the bumper of the rear car attached to the engine, for the purpose of riding. The victim, Charles Gerstner, about 16 years of age, a son of George Gerstner, who was standing near, conceived the idea of standing on the track and as the train came up to swing himself on the car by catching hold of the bumper. He either mistook the speed of the cars or missed his intended hold, and was struck on the shoulder, knocking him down on the track, the car running over his left leg, about half way between the ankle and knee joints, and injuring his arm and head. The train was immediately stopped, but he gave only a few gasps after assistance came, his death being almost instantaneous.

We have seen humanity mutilated in almost every conceivable manner, but we do not remember that we ever saw a more shocking spectacle than poor Charley was when we saw him at his father's house, as he lay stiffening in death on the bed he had so shortly before left with bright prospects of life before him. It was a silent but powerful illustration of the uncertainty of life. The afflicted family have our sympathy in their unexpected bereavement.

We learn that it is a common practice among some of the boys to jump on and off the trains while in motion. If so, this should be a warning to them. Parents, too, should be more particular than they have been in the past. No blame can be attached to the railroad men, as both the fireman and brakeman tried to keep Charley from jumping on the car, but it is supposed that he did not understand them, as his hearing was defective."

Gillam, William H.   b 1 Oct 1856   d 13 Sep 1857   11 m 18 d

William was the son of Rev. N. and S. I was not able to find any definite information about him or his family.

Ginger, Albert F.   b 4 Dec 1847   d 12 Apr 1878   30 y 4 m 8 d

Obituary, Winchester Journal, April 17, 1878:

"DIED__On Friday last, ALBERT F. GINGER, of this city of Consumption, aged 30 years, 4 months and 8 days. Funeral services were held last Sabbath at 2 0'clock p.m. by Elder J.H. Vinson, after which the remains were interred in the cemetery. Both our city Bands and many citizens followed them to their final resting place. The deceased was a quiet unassuming young man and left many friends to mourn his early death."

I did not find any other information about Albert or his family.

Ginther, Henry   b 1866   d 20 Nov 1877   11 y 8 m 3 d

On the 1870 census of Winchester, Anthony Ginther is 45, a potter born in Germany, his wife is Louisa age 38, born in Germany. They have the following children, all born in Indiana: Lucinda, age 12, Frederick, age 9, William, age 6, Henry, age 4 and Minnie, age 7 months.

Obituary, Winchester Journal, November 28, 1877:

"DIED__In this city, on Tuesday, Nov. 20, HENRY GINTHER, son of Mr. and Mrs. A. Ginther, aged about 11 years. Funeral services the following day at the Evangelical Church by Rev. Elkanah Beard."

CHAPTER EIGHT

I AM REBECCA PEARSE GOODRICH, AND I WANT TO TELL YOU MY STORY

Good day to you. My story starts in Virginia in 1789, the year of my birth. My father's name was Baldwin Pearse and both he and my mother were connected with some of the oldest and best families in Virginia. I was fortunate during my childhood to have educational advantages and to be trained in how to manage a home and family while also meeting the expectations of society.

Father was a lawyer and my future husband, John Baldwin Goodrich, joined my father's law practice. We met and fell in love and married. I was only 13 years old at the time of our marriage in 1802 and between 1803 and 1828 we had fourteen children.

John was a very successful man who provided well for our family as both a teacher and a lawyer. At one time he was the president of the Blacksburg Virginia Academy which those now living call the Virginia Polytechnic Institute. We lived well and the children were educated by their father and me.

Then the worst that could possibly happen did happen. In September of 1828 John fell from a horse and was killed. I was 39 years old with 14 children. Thomas, my eldest, was 25. Ten of the children were under the age of 18 and the youngest, baby Charles, was less than a month old.

Our resources quickly diminished without a husband and father to provide for us. Edmund, my second son, was married and along with me took on the role of the family leader. He and I discussed how we could provide for the family in a way that could allow each of them to pursue educational and financial success. There were few chances for that success in Virginia so we chose to move the family west where the prospects were more favorable. John had provided significant culture, education and training for the older children. We brought his fine library of books with us, along with a strong resolve that seemed to be a value of Goodrich's for several generations before us.

We left in December of 1831 after the sale of John's assets. We had about $200. We packed all of the possessions we could on two horse drawn wagons. Our goal was northeastern Indiana, a distance of about 400 miles. The trip was made by Edmund and his wife, Ellen, and their new son, John Baldwin, who was only six weeks old. I, along with Louisa, Jane, Eliza, George and Charles, rode in a wagon. Thomas, Alfred, Calvin and Luther walked alongside. Four of the adult children stayed behind in Virginia and three of those moved to Indiana later.

We reached east-central Indiana in January of 1832. After six weeks of difficult traveling along muddy Indian trails and animal paths, one of our wagons broke down when we attempted to cross the White River. I have been credited with saying, "We'll go no further. One swamp is as good as another." I confess that I did say that.

Indiana had been a state for almost 16 years but it was still thickly wooded and sparsely populated. We were one of several hundred families who came here starting in 1816 and we shared the land with the Miami and Delaware Indians.

Edmund bought a farm adjoining Winchester from a Mormon family that left for Missouri while I bought some land about two miles from town. We first built a log cabin, but in time built a two-story log house that remained our home until all of the children were grown and on their own.

The oldest children were educated while in Virginia and I taught the younger ones. My best fortune was that at the time when many children died, all 14 of my children survived to adulthood and all became successful. Edmund was a lawyer and judge, John studied surveying and math. He loved to travel and ended up in Texas where he was killed by Indians, a sad blow to our family. Carey ran a dry goods store in Virginia, and then joined the family in Winchester where he became a lawyer. Alfred left home young, married and moved to Missouri. George became a master builder and designer, and headed also to Missouri where he had a large family. Eventually he moved back to Peru, Indiana, where he ran a successful mercantile business. Calvin went to Ashbury University and then taught at the County Seminary in Winchester when it opened. He later became a physician and practiced medicine in Ohio, Indiana and finally in Minneapolis, Minnesota. Martin Luther stayed at the homestead the longest but pursued farming in Missouri. Little Charlie started out as a teacher but soon got into commerce and headed a business in Cincinnati.

All of my five daughters were accomplished young ladies who married well. Caroline married Dr. Beverly here in Winchester and died shortly after giving birth. Ann later became Dr. Beverly's second wife. Rebecca also died just a couple of years after marrying. Celestina, the oldest, lived here for quite a while, and then she and her husband moved to Alabama after the Civil War. Jane's husband was a druggist and they moved to Toledo, Ohio. Ann and Jane both attended the Female Institute of Oxford, Ohio, graduating in 1852.

And that little grandson, John Baldwin, who came with us at age 6 weeks to Winchester? He went on to marry and father my great-grandsons who became known as the Goodrich Bothers and who succeeded so well in Winchester.

If you walk around the graveyard you will see only a few headstones for some of the family. Most have been destroyed by time and neglect, and perhaps some vandalism. Thomas Watkins is buried here, as are Carey and his wife, Lydia and three of their four children, Emma, John and Baby. Carolina is also buried here. I have two other grandchildren here also. They are the children of Dr. Beverly, Eldred the son of Caroline and Iris the daughter of Ann. Several of us no longer have gravestones.

I lived a long life filled with the usual elations and sadnesses, successes and struggles. As I look back I am grateful that the wagon broke down. Winchester provided the ideal place for my children to succeed and set the stage for future generations of Goodrich's who also prospered so well in this town.

The Goodrich Family

The Goodrich family has probably had more influence on the City of Winchester than any other family. Descendents still live in Jay and Randolph counties. They are an easy family to research because so much has been written. I took information from Tucker's History of Randolph County, 1882, from the book <u>The Goodriches, An American Family</u> by Dane Starbuck and from material collected at the Randolph County Historical Society Museum. I also found a lot of information on the internet.

The Goodrich family origins are in England. One of three brothers who came from England, Edmund B. Goodrich, settled in Petersburg, Virginia. One of Edmund's sons was named John Baldwin Goodrich, born in Virginia in 1783. He became a lawyer and a teacher. For the purpose of this chapter, I will refer to him as the first John Baldwin Goodrich, though there may be others by that name further back in history. Like many families, they kept naming their male children after fathers, grandfathers and uncles, so it is easy to get lost among the generations of same-named Goodriches.

John Baldwin Goodrich (the first) practiced law with a man named Baldwin Pearse. In 1802 he married the daughter of his law mentor, Rebecca Pearse, who was only 13 years old when they wed. Her story precedes this article. I read somewhere in my research that Rebecca was a very petite woman who never weighed more than 90 pounds.

After John died in the horse accident, the family moved to Winchester. Rebecca relates that quite well in her story, so I will not repeat the details. They arrived in Winchester in 1832, 16 years after Indiana became a state and 14 years after Randolph became a county and Winchester became its county seat.

A married son who came with her, along with his wife and infant son, bought land that is now the Goodrich Park and the land used for Winchester Community High School. Rebecca bought land and built a cabin about two miles west of Winchester. Her remaining underage children were raised and schooled by her in this environment.

Rebecca listed the Goodrich Family members who are buried in the Old Winchester. Most prominent of those is the family matriarch herself, Rebecca Pearse Goodrich. It was of special interest to me that she must have a memorial marker placed. With the last of the money left in the restoration treasury, augmented by a donation from the Goodrich Family Foundation in Jay County, Indiana, a bench has been placed as a memorial to her. You will find it under a tree nearby the gravestones of three of her grandchildren. It's a good place to sit and remember our history.

This is also a good place to thank the family members who make up the Goodrich Family Foundation in Portland, Indiana. They donated money several times during the restoration process. Those donations were significant in helping our committee make the restoration a reality. I, personally, am forever grateful.

The Carey Goodrich Family

If you take a walk through the Old Winchester Graveyard you will come upon the gravestones of three Goodrich children. Their memorials have been restored and are easily readable.

The first one is that of John H., son of C.S. and L.A. Goodrich, born April 25, 1847, and died August 12, 1850. He was three when he died from an unknown cause. When found under the dirt, his stone was in several pieces, but it is now repaired and cleaned. It has a lamb on it (often seen on children's grave markers) and the epitaph reads "Suffer little children to come unto me and forbid them not for such is the kingdom of heaven."

One is simply inscribed "Our Babe", July 12, 1855, C.S. and L.A. Goodrich. From this we know that the baby was either stillborn or died shortly after birth. Like most of the stones, we found this one broken into several pieces.

Beside the other two is Emma Jane Goodrich, daughter of C.S. and L. A. Goodrich who died September 17, 1860, age 8 years, 2 months and 8 days. It is a beautiful stone with carved flowers. The overall condition is excellent. Carved into the stone is the following epitaph "Come to this happy land, come come away. Why will ye doubting stand, why still delay." The cause of Emma's death is not known.

What pain this family must have endured as they lost their children one by one.

The father of the children was Carey Seldon Goodrich, the fourth son of John B. and Rebecca Goodrich When he came to Winchester he entered into a dry goods business with his brother, Edmund. The building housing the business was erected about 1834, was brick and was on the north side of East Washington Street. After a few prosperous years the business dwindled and was closed.

Carey then became a lawyer. In Tucker's 1882 History, Carey is described as a careful manager and a shrewd businessman who accumulated quite a comfortable fortune. He married Lydia Ann Hutton who had family in Richmond. I found little history about Lydia Ann. According to history they had four children, Annie being the only one to survive to adulthood. She married Albert J. Jessup of Winchester. You have already read about the other three.

According to Tucker's History, Carey was very active in the community. He and Lydia were members of the Methodist Episcopal Church. He was described as a "respected, valuable and worthy citizen, deeply interested in the substantial welfare of the community, and earnestly active in every enterprise for its promotion."

The final home of Carey and Lydia was designed by his brother, George an architech, and was built in 1858. This home, located at 416 S. Meridian St., is now occupied by the Randolph County Historical Society Museum.

Carey was born in 1811 and died in 1865 of unknown cause at the age of 54. Lydia Ann Hutton Goodrich was born in 1815 and died in 1869. In her will she named a brother as trustee of the estate because their only surviving child, Annie, was not of age. Both Carey and Lydia are buried in the Old Winchester Graveyard. Their memorial gravestones were not found.

CHAPTER NINE

GORDON, MARY A. – HARVEY, JAMES W.

Gordon, Mary A.　　　b 11 Jul 1847　　　d 4 Jun 1873　　　27 y

Obituary, Winchester Journal, June 18, 1873:

"Died, Jun 4th, 1873, MARY A. GORDON, consort of T. S. Gordon and daughter of Davis and Elizabeth Hutchens. She was born in Winchester, July 11, 1847; went to Jay County in 1862, and taught school there and in Wells County two years, where her services were highly appreciated.

She then attended Liber College two terms, then returned to Winchester, and attended the High School three months. She afterwards taught fifteen months in the primary department of the latter school. I have been told by a worthy gentleman who was connected with the school, that she gave entire satisfaction to teachers, parents and children, and that the attachment found between her and her children was very pleasant. She was firm, affable, kind and affectionate, and esteemed by those who knew her best. She and Mr. Gordon, who taught in the same school, were on the 30th day of May, 1872, united in the state of matrimony. They quit the school room and went to their farm, with prospects and hopes bright for the future. But, alas! In a few weeks she began to feel the effects of the disease which terminated her earthly existence. On the 24th of May, Dr. Howe, of Cincinnati, with six other physicians in attendance, by a surgical operation, removed a tumor from her side that weighed nearly forty pounds. After the operation, hopes were entertained that she would recover; but death had selected its victim and it was beyond the skill of man to turn its shift. Through her affliction she was cheerful, sometimes expressing her desire to live, but was willing to depart if it was the Master's will, believing that her friend's loss would be her gain. The silver cord was loosed, the golden bowl broken and the mourners go about the street. What a happy change when the spirit emerges from its tenement of clay and is borne upon the wings of delight to the transparent mansions of bliss, which Christ went to prepare for the redeemed of the Lord, and there with angels and comrades who passed over before join to sing anthem and doxologies before the throne of God.

Now let me say to those who have been made to drink the bitter cup of grief at the departure of a dear friend, and who wish to associate with her throughout the long day of eternity in the upper coasts of glory. Be ye also ready, have on the wedding garments, have your lamps trimmed and burning and your garments washed and made white in the blood of the Lamb. And buy of Him gold, tried in the fire that ye may be rich." (the rest was not readable on the microfilm)

Groshong, Belinda or   b 1821   d 1849   28 y ?
Melinda or Malinda

Belinda was the wife of Zimri Groshong and the daughter of David and Mary Martin Reeder.

This person was very difficult to research. In some records she was called Malinda, in others, Belinda. To complicate matters she and

Zimri had a daughter named Belinda. After the mother, Belinda, died, husband, Zimri, remarried a lady named Mahala. It was very confusing! I found a one year old named Balinda E. Groshong living with Hannah Way on the 1850 census and wondered if this could be the child of Belinda/Malinda. If anyone reading this book is an ancestor of this family, I invite you to continue the search for historical clarification.

Harrman, Frank   b 13 May 1850   d 21 Mar 1872   21 y 10 m 8 d

Frank is the son of Henry and Philippine.

All four members of the Harrman family are buried together with one grave marker, along with Catherine Fie (Fry), Philippine's mother. The name is spelled Harman on the census. Philippine's name is spelled multiple ways on records. The family came from Germany.

Harrman, Hannah   b 12 Feb 1852   d 2 Mar 1855   3 y 1 m 18 d

Hannah is the daughter of Henry and Philippine according to the tombstone they all share.

Harrman, Henry   b 15 Apr 1811   d 30 Dec 1880   69 y 1 m 18 d

On the 1860 census Henry is 49, Philippine is 50, Henry Jr. is 24, Adam is 22, Mary is 15, Nicholas is 10, Frank is 8, Elizabeth is 6 and Caroline is 4.

On the 1870 census of White River Township, Randolph County, Henry is a farmer, age 58. His wife, Philippine is 60, Nicholas is 21, Frank is 19, Liza is 16 and Caroline is 13.

Obituary, Winchester Journal, January 5, 1881:

"DIED__On Thursday last, Henry Harmon, Sr, after a short illness of lung fever. The deceased was nearly 70 years old and had resided in this county for many years. His remains were interred on Friday with the honors of Masonry.

A copy of his will is available at the Randolph County Historical Society Museum.

The family had thirteen children so it is probable that others may also be buried at the Old Winchester Graveyard, but just the one gravestone was found.

Harmann, Philippine   b 9 Dec 1809   d 13 Apr 1878   68 y 4 m 4 d

Obituary, Winchester Journal, April 17, 1878:

"DIED__Mrs. Phillipena Harmon, wife of Henry Harman, died on Friday evening last, aged 68 years, 3 months and 4 days, after an illness of several months. Rev. Mr. Brewer preached an appropriate sermon last Sabbath afternoon at the German church, after which the remains were laid away in the cemetery. She was buried by New Dayton Grange with the honors of that order. Mrs. H. was the mother of 13 children, 6 of whom are living. She leaves a husband, children, 24 grandchildren and many other friends to mourn her death. She was a sister of Mrs. Thomas Klinck of this place."

Harvey, James W.   b 11 May 1812   d 17 Jun 1875   63 y

James was married to Louisa H. Porterfield on June 19, 1843, in Preble County, Ohio.

On the 1850 census in Preble County, James W. was 38, Louisa H. was 38 and they had two children, Thomas, age 8 and George B., age 2.

Louisa died in 1852 and is likely buried in Ohio.

Obituary, Winchester Journal, June 23, 1875:

"Sudden Death-James W. Harvey, a shoemaker in the employ of Charles Woolverton, died very suddenly of Heart Disease, at the residence of Elder Morrison on Meridian Street last Thursday evening. The deceased had been working as usual during the day, and after supper he and wife went to Mr. Morrison's, with whose family they were intimate. Soon after starting from home, Mr. H. complained of a severe pain in his breast, and his wife suggested that they return home, but he thought the pain was merely temporary and they went on. Soon after reaching Mr. M's., Harvey laid down on the lounge, and died almost instantly without a struggle. The deceased has resided here for three or four years past, and was a little over 63 years old at the time of his death. He was a consistent member of the Christian Church, and we believe was fully prepared to meet his God. He was a kind, unobtrusive gentleman, and was liked by all who knew him. Funeral services were held by Elder Morrison at the Christian Church Friday evening, after which the remains were interred in the cemetery.

The deceased was born near New Paris, Ohio, May 11, 1812, where he lived most of his life. He was married to Louisa Porterfield in 1843. His first wife died in 1852, leaving one child, Thos. H. Harvey, who is the only child of the deceased and now lives at Emporia, Kansas. He married Phebe A. Dunham on June, 3, 1853 with whom he has lived happily ever since. He joined the Christian Church at New Paris in 1835 and has lived a faithful Christian life ever since. He was a quiet, unassuming and kind-hearted man. He was always of that even temper which comes to those who follow peace with all men. He taught the great lesson of Christianity by an upright walk and a godly conversation among men."

His obituary states that he was left with only one child, Thomas H. It is likely that George, who is age two on the 1850 census, died and is buried in Ohio.

CHAPTER TEN

THE HEASTON FAMILY

Heaston, Catherine	b 1791	d 9 Aug 1876	85 y
Heaston, David	b 1793	d 18 Dec 1865	72 y

The Heastons of Randolph County are descendents of John and Mary Ann Heaston. Both came from Germany and settled in Rockingham County, Virginia. Mary Ann died young and John went back to Germany, married his deceased wife's sister and returned to Virginia. His second wife died after a short marriage and for his third wife John married a native of Pennsylvania and moved with his new wife and children to Ohio. According to Tucker's History, David was the fourth of seven children, so at least four of them were the children of John and Mary Ann.

This tribute is written about the son of John and Mary Ann, who was born in Virginia in 1793. When David was nine he moved with his family to Montgomery County, Ohio. They lived on a farm and endured all of the deprivations and hardships of pioneer life. He had limited educational opportunities, attending school for only 14 days during his life. But his father was a highly educated man who taught school for many years, so David and his siblings were probably taught at home. Tucker's 1882 History of Randolph County describes David as "a fair scholar in literature and an excellent accountant, the result of self-education."

David joined the army during the War of 1812 and was engaged against the Indians on the Western frontier until the close of the war. A military monument in his honor has been placed in the graveyard.

In 1817, David married Catherine Pressel, the daughter of Daniel and Magdaline (Ledy) Pressel. David worked in a distillery in Dayton for two years, then he and Catherine and their newborn daughter moved to Randolph County, arriving on Christmas Day, 1819.

David bought 160 acres of unimproved land three miles south of Winchester. He later sold that and bought 140 acres with a log cabin and several cleared acres. He continued to buy up land until he had 640 acres. By every standard of the day, the Heastons, through hard work and persistence, became wealthy people.

His wife, Catherine, must have been highly regarded because she is one of only a few women who had a biography written in Tucker's history. She and David were the parents of four children: Mary Ann (Wright), Nathaniel P., Lewis L. and David Jr., who died in 1833. According to Tucker

"Mr. Heaston was noted for his kindness of heart and liberality, especially toward the poor and unfortunate. His hand and heart were ever open to supply their wants, and it is said he never turned the hungry away from his door. In addition to their own family, Mr. and Mrs. Heaston raised and educated five persons. His wife was a woman of small stature, but of strong constitution, and was of indispensable service to her husband in their pioneer life. Mr. and Mrs. Heaston were honored and exemplary citizens of the country and none know them but to love and respect them."

David is important to the history of the Old Winchester Graveyard because he donated the original 77 lots for the cemetery and gave it to the town of Winchester. It was opened in 1844 but there were burials that took place earlier than that date. A.J. Neff added 36 lots a few years later. A second Heaston addition was added with 126 lots. The total graveyard had 239 lots, each of them able to hold 6-8 burial sites. The potential is that about 1500 people were buried there, but without any written records we will never know.

General Asahel Stone bought land from David Heaston to build his home and also bought land from David's brother, Christian Heaston, to develop the Fountain Park Cemetery. After the opening of Fountain Park, it became common language to refer to the Heaston Cemetery as the "Old Winchester Graveyard." While we casually call it the "Old Winchester," you will find the name Heaston on the signs in recognition of its correct historical name.

According to Tucker's history there seemed to be little going on in the county and in Winchester in which David and Catherine were not involved. In 1828 David was a tax collector. In 1838, he was one of the signers incorporating Winchester as a town; and he did some work on the second courthouse, for which he was paid $109.67. In 1840 he signed a petition against businesses selling intoxicating drink. He is listed as a coroner in Winchester and in 1858 he exhibited "a beautiful Durham cow" at the Agricultural Fair in Winchester. Early on, he bought Winchester's first courthouse and used it as a hotel. Later, he sold it to Paul Way who was proprietor for many years. He made a speech at the first meeting of the "Old Settlers", in 1861.

David Heaston died December 18, 1865 at the age of 71 and is buried in his graveyard. Catherine died August 9, 1876 at the age of 85 and is buried with David. Their gravestones were not found. Their infant grandson, Edward Wright, is buried there also. His stone has been restored.

David and Catherine have a large monument in their memory at the Fountain Park Cemetery, but there is no record that their remains were moved there. In the restoration process we found stones in both places because there was concern about the poor maintenance of the Old Winchester and families wanted to make sure a grave-stone was placed in their family member's honor and memory. I am certain that David and Catherine lie buried somewhere in their graveyard, in unmarked graves.

On the 1850 census of White River Township, Randolph County, David is 56 and a farmer, Catherine is listed as 54, and they are listed with two of their children; Nathaniel age 25, a surveyor and Lewis, age 23, a farmer. Obviously, there is an error in the age for Catherine. I found information on the Heastons from multiple sources and both of them had different birth and death dates in different sources, but in each case they were close. This is another example of the inconsistency of old records.

Obituary, Winchester Journal, August 16, 1876:

"Aunt Katie Heaston, as she was familiarly known, relict of the late David Heaston, died at Edward Wright's last Wednesday. The deceased was one of the pioneers of the county and was loved by all who knew her."

CHAPTER ELEVEN

HEIKS, LAURA-NEFF, INFANT

Heiks, Laura   b ?   d 1875   ? y

Along with mentioning a Mr. Dye in a Winchester Journal article written on September 22, 1875, the writer also mentioned the newly arranged gravesite of Laura Heiks. It was also noted that a Mr. J. Heiks was clearing some of the brush from the cemetery and had greatly improved the appearance.

I was not able to find any information about Laura, or her father, Mr. J Heiks.

Hill, Lottie   b 15 Nov 1848   d 14 Nov 1876   28 y

Obituary, Winchester Journal, November 22, 1876:

> "Died at her residence, near Winchester, November 14th, of heart disease, Lottie, wife of B.F. Hill. She was born in Randolph County November 15, 1848, age 28 years. Mrs. Hill was a member of the M.E. Church, and died in the hope of a blessed immortality. She leaves a husband, three children and many relatives and friends to mourn her sad death. Funeral services were conducted by John A. Hunt at Cerro Gordo. The remains were interred in the Winchester Cemetery."

Hinson, Jacob   b 1837   d 5 Dec 1848   11 y

Jacob was the son of John and N. I could not find any information on this family.

Houk, Nancy E.   b 22 May 1830 d 1 Jul 1869   39 y 2 m 9 d

On the 1860 census of White River Township, Randolph County, M.H. Houk is 23, a farmer, Nancy E. is 30 and they have two children, Lanora, age 8 and James H., age 1.

In November of 1869, Michael married Sarah Ann Cox, who was a widow with children. On the 1870 census Michael is 37, Sarah is 44, Lanora is 14, James is 11 and Willie is 9. Sarah's children are Alva Cox age 14, William age 11 and Angela age 7. I am not sure whose child Willie is, but am sure his age is not correct, nor is Lanora's.

On www. findagrave.com, I found Michael buried at New Dayton Cemetery in Farmland. He had served in Co. K., 40th Ohio Infantry.

Houser, James   b ?   d ?   ? y

I was able to find some Housers in Winchester. James could be the child of Jonathan and Susannah Houser who resided in White River Township on the 1870 census, or he could be their grandchild. He may be a son or brother to Eli, Daniel, or George.

Hull, Elizabeth   b 1824   d 28 Jun 1853   29 y 6 m 1 d

Hull, William W.   b 16 Aug 1819 d 1 May 1851   31 y 8 m 16 d

Hull, Jehiel (J.R.)   b 1846   d ?   ? y

Elizabeth Wysong was married in Randolph County on January 15, 1845 to William W. Hull.

Elizabeth is the daughter of Valentine and Elizabeth Albright Wysong, both of German descent. She is one of nine children. I was not able to link William W. to a specific family. However, there were two Jehiel Hulls, one the right age to be William's father, and the other listed as his son on the 1850 census. The older Jehiel Hull was also a brick mason. This was a confusing family to pin down.

On the 1850 census of Cambridge City, Wayne Co., Indiana, William is 31 and a brick mason, Elizabeth is 24 and they have two children, Jehiel, age 4 and Mary E., age 1.

Jehiel (the younger) was in Co. A. 134th Indiana Infantry during the Civil War. He enlisted May 24, 1864 as a private and mustered out on September 2, 1864 at Indianapolis. His military stone was found but was in poor condition, so a new stone was placed for him. There is also a marker for Jehiel in Fountain Park Cemetery, although I did not find any documentation of his remains being moved. He is maintained on the list of both cemeteries.

I found a marriage record in Randolph County for Jehiel Hull to Hannah Bower on October 24, 1868.

William and Elizabeth both died young, two years apart from each other, of unknown causes. I really encourage the reader to visit William's restored gravestone. It is unusual and depicts a bereaved widow standing at her husband's gravesite. It is one of my favorite gravestones.

| **Hull, John Sr.** | b 1 May 1766 | d 2 Aug 1849 | 83 y |
| **Hull, Phebe** | b 1773 | d 19 Aug 1849 | 76 y |

John and Phebe have the earliest birth dates of anyone found buried in the cemetery. They lived a long time and died within days of each other. The U.S. Federal Mortality Record states that both of them died of cholera. I do not know if they are related to William above. I could not find a direct link.

Humphries, Infant   b 1885   d 24 Aug 1885   4 m

This was a child of John and Ann Darrah Humphries.

Death Notice, Winchester Journal, August 26, 1885:

> "The four months old babe of Johnny Humphries died Monday and was buried at the old cemetery yesterday afternoon."

In the Indiana Marriage Collection, Randolph County, I found John Humphries marrying Ann Darrah by Justice of the Peace, Alonzo H. Patty on August 28, 1881.

Huston, John   b 1784   d 11 May 1849   65 y

Huston, Nancy (Snodgrass)   b 1793   d 2 May 1869   76 y

There is a family tree on ancestry.com that lists two children for this couple, Margaret Ewing Huston born is 1831 and James Ewing Huston born in 1837. I cannot verify this information nor did I find anything else about this family.

Hutchens, Josiah   b 1800   d ?   ? y

Hutchens, Hannah Davis   b 1801   d 1881   80 y

Josiah and Hannah married in 1820. On the 1840 census of White River Township, Randolph County, Josiah is listed with the following family members: 1 male age 5-10, 2 males age 15-20, 1 male 30-40 (Josiah), 2 females under age 5, 1 female 10-15 and 1 female 30-40 (Hannah).

I did not find other information about this family.

Irvin, Mary (Banty)   b 24 Mar 1808   d 16 Mar 1843   35 y

Mary was the first wife of Robert Irvin. They married April 29, 1825, in Montgomery County, Ohio. According to a family history on ancestry.com, Robert and Mary had the following children: Mary A., Evaline, Margaret, Louisa, John, Minerva, Eliza, Rosa Ann, Caroline and Robert Rives, the youngest being born four months before Mary died.

Irvin, Robert   b 29 Aug 1805   d 13 Oct 1875   70 y

Robert was the son of John Irvin and Margaret Wysong. He married for a second time in 1844 to Hannah D. Bishop, who was born in 1821. They are listed as having the following children: Lanis, Lamartine, Gertrude, George, Clementine, James, Willard and Jefferson, the youngest being born in 1858. Altogether Robert fathered 17 children with his two wives.

On the census in White River Township, Randolph County in 1850, Robert is 45 and a farmer, Hannah is 29, John 21, Minerva 17, Eliza 15, Rosa A. 13, Caroline 11, Robert 9, Gertrude 5, George 3 and Charles 1.

On the 1860 census in White River Township Robert is 55 and a farmer, Hannah is 38, Gertrude 15, George 18, Charles 11, Lamartine 9, James 7, Willard 4 and Jefferson 2.

On the 1870 census of White River Township, Robert is farming, Hannah is 48, George is 28 and listed as a farm laborer, Lamartine is 19, James 18, Willard 14 and Jefferson 12.

Jarrett, Carrie   b 1870   d 16 Jul 1873   3 y

Carrie was the daughter of William and Emily Reed Jarrett and the granddaughter of Nathan Reed. On the 1870 census of White River Township, Randolph County, William is 27 and a farmer, Emily is 26 and Carrie is 7 months.

Jarrett, Baby   b 1873   d 16 Jul 1873   4 m

Obituary, Winchester Journal, March 19, 1873: "CHILD FOUND DEAD IN BED"

On Thursday morning past, David Jarrett, who lives in the north part of town, found his little four months old child dead. Coroner Grooms was sent for and held an inquest. Drs. Smith and Evans held a post mortem and found that the child had come to its death by suffocation caused by a fungus growth in its throat. The jury returned a verdict that the child came to its death by suffo-cation by a visitation of God and not by violence."

Mrs. Emma Jarrett   b 1843   d 26 Feb 1872   29 y 4 m

Emily was the wife of William and the daughter of Nathan Reed.

Notice, Winchester Journal, February 21, 1872:

"Mrs. Emma Jarrett, daughter of Nathan Reed is lying at the resi-dence of her father very low. Her recovery is doubtful. Mrs. Reed is also confined to her bed."

Obituary,Winchester Journal, February 28, 1872,

"DIED__In this city, on Monday last. Mrs. Emily Jarrett, aged 25 years. Mrs. Jarrett has been a sufferer for four months, but hopes of her recovery were entertained until a short time before her death. A funeral discourse was preached at the M.E. Church by Rev. Mr. Walker yesterday, and the remains escorted to the cemetery by a large concourse of people. Mrs. Jarrett leaves a husband and two small children and many relatives and friends to mourn her death."

Emily (Emma) has a restored memorial marker at the Old Winchester, but is also on the list at Fountain Park Cemetery, so she is one of those maintained on both lists. I think her remains are in the old cemetery, but before her father died he bought multiple lots at Fountain Park and family placed her name on one of them as a memorial.

I found information indicating that William, father of Carrie and husband of Emily, died in 1878 at the age of 36 years of unknown cause, and is buried at Buena Vista Cemetery in Randolph County.

Johnson, Edna Mae   b 20 May 1883   d 13 Sep 1883   3 m 23 d

Edna Mae was the daughter of Manashe and Mahala Johnson. No further information was found for this family.

Jones, Harriett, N.   b 1819   d 18 Feb 1873   54 y 10 m 25 d

On the 1870 census of Winchester, Harriett is 50 and head of household. In the same household are ? Jones (can't read) age 14, male, Charles W., age 10, Laura, age 3, William Brice, age 36 and Emily Brice, age 27.

Obituary, Winchester Journal, February 16, 1873:

"Departed this life, February, 1873, Mrs. Harriet N. Jones, in the 54th year of her age. The deceased was a member of the M.E.

Church. She joined the Cumberland Presbyterian Church in Athens County, Ohio, over thirty-five years ago. After removing to this state and finding no church of her own, she joined the Methodist Church. From the time of her first connection with the Church, until the day of her death, she witnessed a good profession. She loved Christ and drew her comforts from Him. Her happiness was found in communion with him. For many years her life was a suffering and sorrowful one. But she was never known to murmur or complain of her lot. Her many afflictions served to wean her from the world and bring her nearer to God. She is now delivered from sufferings and in a world where there will be no separation of friends, no sickness, and where she is admitted to the immediate presence of her Savior and her God."

In her will Harriett leaves $50 to a daughter, Harriett N. Gwinner, $25 to daughter, Mary E. Connett, $25 to her son, Otho T. Jones and the balance of entire estate after payment of personal expenses to be equally divided between her son, Charles, and her granddaughter, Laura Bell Jones, daughter of Xerxes A. Jones, deceased.

Jones, Thomas W. O.   b 1850   d 5 Aug 1864   14 y 4 m 17 d

Thomas was a son of Thomas W. and Harriett N. Jones. Cause of death is unknown.

Jones, Thomas W.   b 1813?   d 1867 ?   54?

On the 1850 census of White River Township, Randolph County, Thomas W is 38 and a wagon maker, Harriett is 32, Xerxes A. is 11, Mary E. is 10, Q.B. is 8, Harriett R. is 3 and T.W.O. is 4 months.

On the 1860 census Thomas is 48, Harriett N. is 38, Harriett R. is 12, Thomas W.O. is 10, Ortho is 6 and Charles is 9 months.

Jones, Thomas W.   b 1869   d 19 Feb 1873   4 y

This child is the son of Obedidum and Mary Jones. On the 1870 census of Winchester, Obedidum is 28 and a common laborer, his wife Mary is 40, Thomas W. is 1. Also in the household are John E. Rady 18, Patrick Rady 5 and Winfield Rady 1. They seem to be a completely different family of Jones, unrelated to the others listed here.

Jones, Xerxes   b 1839   d pre- 1873   30-35 y

Xerxes was a soldier during the Civil War. He enlisted as a private on August 13, 1862, transferred into Regiment U.S. Veteran Reserve Corps on March 17 1864 and transferred out the same day. His original military marker was found and restored. A new military marker was also set.

Little was found about Xerxes, but I did find an obituary for his wife, who died sometime before Xerxes.

Obituary, Randolph Journal, December 30, 1866:

"Departed this life, at Lynn, on the 20th of November, 1866, Mrs. Laura Jones, consort of Mr. Xerxes A. Jones. The deceased was born at Washington, Davies County, Indiana on May 15, 1838, consequently her age at the day of her death was 28 years, 6 months and fourteen days. We have reason to believe that at a very early period in life, she had serious impressions, convictions of her lost state, and felt her need of an interest in the atoning blood of Christ. Those impressions and feelings continued with her more or less until the month of February, 1862, when she was enabled to surrender her heart to the Savior, and found peace in believing. She at once decided to make an open confession of her attachment to Christ; and this she did by uniting with the

M.E. Church at Merome, in this state, in February, 1862, and from that time until the day of her death she continued to 'adorn the doctrine of her God and Savior in all things: recommending by her example and life that religion of her Savior, which she professed and loved'.

She was naturally kind and amiable and was esteemed and loved by all who knew her. Her end was peace. She met death without dismay. The sting of death was taken away. Her sins were all cancelled, blotted out and she had peace with God through Jesus Christ.

Our sympathies are with the bereaved husband and friends. If she whom you mourn is gone, sleeps in Jesus Christ, lives. He is the same compassionate Friend that wept at the grave of Lazarus, and able and willing to comfort and sustain you in all your afflictions; and moreover, He has only taken away the one for whom you mourn to the full enjoyment of a love more tender than all earthly loves, to a world where tears are never shed, and where sickness and death never come."

Kayser, Julia   b 10 May 1827   d 21 Nov 1878   51 y 6 m 10 d

Obituary, Winchester Journal, November 26, 1878:

"DIED__ In this city, on Thursday last, November 21, 1878, Mrs. Julia Kayser, wife of Christian Kayser. The deceased was born in Grossteinheim, Germany, May 10, 1827. She had been in poor health for many years, caused by lung disease, and had suffered long and patiently. The immediate cause of her death was dropsy. She was an estimable lady, quiet and unobtrusive in her deportment. She was a member of the German Evangelical

Church for many years and died in the hope of a blessed immortality. Funeral services were held at the German Church in
this city last Saturday, by Red. Philip Bretch , who delivered a
very appropriate sermon in the German language, after which
her remains were deposited in the cemetery in the presence of a
large concourse of people."

Keener, Aaron   b 1847   d 31 Dec 1873   26 y 8 m 8 d

Aaron was the son of Nicholas and Catherine Keener.

Winchester Journal,, August 13, 1873:

"Aaron Keener was arrested on Monday last for hunting on the
Sabbath. After a short interview with Squire Reed, Aaron contributed $1 to the School Fund."

Death Notice, Winchester Journal, November 5, 1873:

"Aaron Keener, a young man about 26 years of age, died of Heart
Disease, at the residence of his father, near the water station on
the Bee Line, west of town, on Saturday last. He was buried in
the cemetery near this place, on Sunday last."

Keener, Catherine   b 15 Oct 1825   d 25 Apr 1895   70 y

Catherine was the wife of Nicholas.

A partial obituary was found on microfilm from the Winchester
newspaper published around the time of her death:

"KEENER__Mrs. Cathrine Keener was born in Lebanon Co. Pa., October 15, 1825, departed this life, at her home northwest of this city, April 25, 1895, aged sixty-nine years, six months and ten days. The deceased was married to Nicholas Keener, her now bereaved husband, November 26, 1846, to which union were born five sons and eight daughters, of whom two sons and one daughter preceded her...(unable to read rest of obit)

Keener, Jacob   b 27 Oct 1812   d 22 Nov 1884   72 y 10 m 5 d

Jacob came to the United States from Germany a few years after his brother, Nicholas, and lived with Nicholas and his family most of his life. I found no evidence that he ever married.

In Jacob's will, dated 14 Nov 1883, recorded 29 Nov, 1884, Bk 3 pp 166-67, Randolph County "to brother, Nicholas Keener, all real estate; at his death to go to his heirs."

Keener, Nicholas   b 15 Oct 1815   d 9 Jul 1897   81 y m 26 d

On the 1850 census in Jefferson Township, Franklin County, Ohio, Nicholas is 35 and a tailor, Catherine is 25, Elizabeth is 7, Louisa is 5, Aaron is 3 and Emaline is 1. Jacob Keener, brother to Nicholas, is listed as 39 and a laborer.

On the 1870 census of White River Township, Randolph County, Nicholas is 54 and a farmer, Catherine is 45, David is 20, Mary is 18, Carolina is 14, Abigail is 6, John is 5, Charles is 3 and Aaron is 23 and a laborer.

On the 1880 census Nicholas is 60, Catherine is 50, Abbie is 17, John is 14, Charley is 12, and Jacob is 65.

Notice that again the ages are inconsistent. I write them as they appear on the census report.

Obituary, Winchester newspaper, July 13, 1897:

"KEENER-Nicholas, son of Peter and Susan Keener, was born in Bavaria, Germany, October 15, 1815, died at his home near Winchester, July 9, 1897; aged eighty-one years, eight months and twenty-six days. He came to America in 1837 and settled in Franklin County, Ohio, where he was married to Catharine Dove in 1843, and in 1865 they came to Indiana where they have since resided. Thirteen children blessed this union, five sons and eight daughters; three sons and one daughter have passed on before. The remaining children mourn the loss of a kind and affectionate father. The mother and wife departed this life more than two years ago. Funeral services were held at the East Street Christian Church in this city Sunday morning, conducted by Rev. A.M. Addington, assisted by J.A. Wetzel. Interment was at the cemetery in the south-west portion of Winchester."

In his will Nicholas requested that a stone be erected at the grave of his deceased wife Catherine. To his daughter, Emma Fisher, he willed $100 in appreciation of her care of testator in his old age. Other children named in the will were David, John H., Charles Keener, son-in-law Zimroe Wright and son-in-law James Jarrett. He requested that his estate be divided to be shared by all his named children including the above named plus Malinda Jarrett, Elizabeth Wright, Louisa Keener, Mary Dennis, Caroline Fisher, Abigail Booher and grandson Lewis Keener, son of Charles M. Keener.

Keller, Rosina   b 11 Mar 1859   d ?   ? y

Keller, Maria   b 27 Jul 1860   d ?   ? y

Keller, Johan Heinrich   b 15 Aug 1861   d ?   ? y

Keller, Christian Franklin   b 9 Jul 1865   d ?   ? y

These are the children of George Gottfred Keller and Catharine Elizabeth Kayser Keller who came from Germany. The graves were placed near the west end of the cemetery according to Irene Brumfield. She is now deceased but left notes with staff at the Randolph County Historical Society that she had visited their gravesites. I am unable to confirm Mrs. Brumfield's information with any other documentation but have every reason to believe it is reliable.

On the 1860 census of White River Township, Randolph County, George G. Keller is 32 and a shoemaker. His wife, Catharine, is 32 and they have children George, age 7, Catharine, age 5, Charles, age 4 and Juliann, age 2.

On the 1870 census of Winchester, George is 42 and a retail grocer, Catharine is 42, George is 16, Charles is 14, Catharine is 15, Julia is 12, Henry is 8 and Frank is 1.

On the 1880 census G.G. Keller is 52 and a retail grocer, Catharine is 53, Charles is 24, Julia is 22, Henry is 18 and Franklin is 11.

Kelley, Jemima   b 1782   d 18 Mar 1855   73 y

Her tombstone says that she is the wife of Jacob.

On the 1850 census of White River Township, Randolph County, Jemima is the head of household listed as age 74 (has to be error since different than tombstone, must have been 69), listed with John Kelley age 28, a farmer and probably a son.

No other information was found.

Kinney, Susanah   b 1860   d 16 Feb 1877   17 y 4 m 11 d

Obituary, Winchester Journal, February 21, 1877:

"DIED__Susanah Kinney, wife of George Kinney, Feb. 16, 1877 aged 17 years 11 months and 4 days. The deceased connected herself with the M. E. Church, sometime this winter, and died in the triumph of a living faith. Funeral on the 17th by Rev. T.W. Thornburg at Kizer's Chapel."

Lavin, Sophie (Martin)   b 1840   d 31 Sep 1855   15 y 7 m 10 d

She is listed as the wife of Michael and the daughter of J. and S. Martin.

On the 1850 census of Monroe Township, Randolph County, Joseph is 56, a farmer, Susana is 49, Samuel is 21, Elizabeth is 20, Rachael is 15, Rosana is 12, Catherine and Sophie are both 10, Susana is 8 and Noah is 6.

Lavin, Infant   b 1855   d 31 Sep 1855   newborn

Lavin, Michael   b ?   d 14 Jul , 1872   ? y

Marriage record of Randolph County, January 4, 1855, Michael Lavin to Sophia Martin by John B. Marl.

There were several others named Lavin living in the area, all from Ireland, assumed to be relatives.

Article, Winchester Journal, July 17, 1872:

"ANOTHER RAILROAD HORROR. One of our Citizens Killed and Another Badly Wounded. Another railroad accident occurred on the 'Bee Line' near Fortville, in Hancock County, on Friday evening last, in which an Irishman named Michael Lavin, a resident of this place, was so badly injured that he died two days after. Henry Gardiner, 'boss' of the extra gang of track hands, also a resident of this place, was severely injured. The gang had quit work for the day and were going to Fortville for the night, using three handcars, following each other closely and running at a high rate of speed. By some means, one of the hands on the front car lost his balance and fell off in front of the second car on the front end, of which Gardiner was riding. As this car approached the man, Gardiner reached out to push him off of the track, when he lost his balance and fell off, the car running over both of his legs. This checked the speed of that car, and the third car, not noticing what had happened, came rushing along full speed, also running over Gardiner and struck the second car and mangling Lavin, who was riding on the rear of the second car with his feet hanging over. Several others were injured, but we were unable to get their names. Gardiner and Lavin were both brought home on Saturday. Lavin died Sunday night, but Gardiner is getting along finely and will be able to be out in a few days."

Lennon, Elizabeth   b 27 Aug 1859   d 16 Sep 1860   1 y 4 m 20 d

Elizabeth was the daughter of Dennis and Susannah (Martin). At findagrave.com, I found the following children listed for Dennis and Susannah, both of whom are buried at Fountain Park Cemetery: Elizabeth (died age 1), Edward, Charles, Anna, Jennie, Mary, Emma, Frank and John Patrick.

Lewelling, William   b 10 Sep 1868   d 23 Jun 1870   1 y 9 m3 d
(Willie) E.

On the 1870 census of Winchester, Henry C. is 26 and a carpenter, Ester is 25, and their children are Emma C., age 5, Elva E., age 4, and William E., age 1.

Henry served as a private in the 133rd Indiana Infantry for 100 days in 1864.

Mace, Cynthia   b 23 Oct 1833   d 21 Mar 1868   43 y 5 m 28 d

On the 1860 census of White River Township, Randolph County, James Mace is 38 and a farmer, and Cynthia is 27. No children are listed. No other information was found.

Manderbach, Leo   b 1 Apr 1860   d 31 May 1862   1 y 11 m 30 d

Leo was the baby son of William A. and M.A.

On the 1860 census of Nettle Creek Township, Randolph County, William is listed as age 26, a baker from Germany, M. Ann is 22, born in Pennsylvania and Leo is 1, born in Indiana.

On the 1870 census of Winchester, William is 36, a grocer/baker, Annie is 33, Cassie is 9, Henry is 6, William is 5, John is 3 and Liza is 1.

Martin, Elisha J.   b 31 Aug 1862   d 7 Jun 1868   5 y 9 m 7 d

Martin, Male Child   b ?   d 16 Aug 1876   ? y

They were the sons of O. and J.

On the 1860 census of White River Township, Randolph County, Oliver Martin is 28, Julia A. is 25, David S. is 5, Sarah A. is 3 and Henrietta R. is 8 months.

On the 1850 census in White River Township, Oliver is 18 and living with his parents, Elisha and Susannah Martin and seven siblings. Probably our little Elisha is named after his grandpa.

Oliver Martin and Julia Livingston were married in Randolph County on July 1, 1854.

Oliver and Julia both died in January, 1907, a week apart from each other, Julia on the 13th and Oliver on the 20th. They were 71 and 74 years of age.

Martin, Elizabeth (Romizer)   b 1815   d 9 Jun 1874   50 y

Elizabeth was the wife of Joseph and was born in Parmasen, Rhein, Bavaria.

Martin, Elizabeth   b 1 Mar 1828   d 14 Apr 1852   24 y 1 m 14 d

Martin, Joseph   b 4 Mar 1797   d 5 Jun 1871   71 y ?

Joseph was married three times. Nancy Miller was his first wife and they married February 26, 1818. He married next Susannah Miller on June 5, 1823. His third wife was Elizabeth Romizer whom he married October 7, 1852.

Nancy, who died in 1822 in Pennsylvania was probably the mother of David.

Susannah was probably the mother of Samuel, Elizabeth (listed above as deceased, age 24), Abigail, Rachel, Rosanna, Sophie (listed under Lavin), Catherine, Susannah and Noah.

Children with Elizabeth Romizer (listed above) were: Mary, Patrick, Eliza and Emma.

Obituary, Winchester Journal, June 21, 1871:

"DIED__In this city, on Thursday last, June 15, Mr. Joseph Martin, in the 67th year of his life. Mr. M. has been an invalid for some time. He was struck with palsy almost two years ago, since which time he has been almost totally helpless. He had another stroke the evening just prior to his death, from the effects of which he never rallied, but lay unconscious until death relieved him. Mr. M. was a German by birth, quiet and unostentatious in manners, and had been until his condition a very industrious man. He leaves a wife and several children."

The dates on the two Elizabeth Martins are taken from their restored grave markers in the Old Graveyard. On ancestry.com someone doing Joseph's genealogy listed Joseph as being born in Germany, as having three wives and many children. All of the children listed above do appear on census reports of 1850, 1860 and/or 1870, but the ages are always slightly off, so it is confusing at best. We did not find a stone for Joseph, but Tucker's history book lists him as buried at the Old Winchester so we consider that reliable information. But again, the dates do not match. Perhaps there are descendents who will get it all figured out.

May, Jessie, Capt.   b 1836   d 1866   30 y

Jessie's name is also spelled Jesse on military records. He was commissioned as an officer on March 5, 1864, was promoted to Full Captain on January 1, 1865, and mustered out on August 31, 1865 at Greensboro, NC.

He died the next year of an unknown cause at age 30.

On the 1860 census of White River Township, Randolph County, Charles May is 45, Mary is 46, Jesse is 24, Mary 18, Elizabeth 20, Sarah J. 16, Eliza E. 13, Charles 11, Rebecca J. 9, Amanda 7 and Gilly 6.

McConochy, America   b 1838   d 31 Dec 1866   28 y 9 m 9 d

Marriage record, Randolph County, April 9, 1859: Daniel McConochy to America Pugh.

On the 1850 census of White River Township, Randolph County, America is living with her birth family: Ellis Pugh age 49 and a farmer, Mary, age 42, William, 21, Addison, 19, Nathanie,l 17, Morris, 15, America ,12 and Leander, 4.

On the 1860 census of White River Township, Daniel McConochy is 20, a farmer, America is 22 and they have a baby, Mary E., age 8 months.

McLeaf, Mr.   b ?   d ?   ? y

Please refer to an article from the Winchester Journal of September 22, 1875 that is written out in full under Mr. Dye. No information was found about Mr. McLeaf.

Meier, Nora   b 2 Apr 1880   d 2 Apr 1880   newborn twins
Charlotta

Meier, Norwood K.

Nora and Norwood were newborn twins of Johan Conrad Meier and Catherine Elizabeth Keller and are siblings to Irene Brumfield (deceased) who provided the information. She reported to members of the Randolph County Historical Society that memorial stones for the infants were still in the cemetery in the 1960's. Both parents were from Germany.

In 1880, when the babies died, John C. was 30 and a baker, C.E. was 2 and they had Alice, age 5.

In the 1900 census of White River Township, Randolph County, John C. was 50, a baker, Catherine E. was 45, Hugo H. was 18, Edwin J. was 15, Alma A. was 12, Irene L. was 10, Clifford was 7 and Robert was 2.

By the 1920 census, John was 69 and a retired baker, Catherine was 65, Alma was 32 and Irene was 30.

Miller, Mary Ann   b 28 Jan 1826   d 22 Dec 1879   53 y 10 m 26 d

On the 1870 census of Winchester, William is 51 and a carpenter, Mary A. is 44 and their children are Mary C. age 21, Marcus age 19 and David S. age 15.

Obituary, Winchester Journal, January 7, 1880:

"Mary Ann Miller, the deceased, was the daughter of William and Nancy Hobbs. She was born in Wayne County, Indiana, January 28, 1826. Her father moved to Shelby County and afterwards to Randolph County, where she married to her present bereaved husband, William Miller, March 25th A.D. 1841. She was the mother of seven children, 3 sons and 4 daughters, 4 of whom are still living, 3 have died. She united with the M.E. Church in Winchester in the great revival of 1856-57. In 1867 she united with the Christian Church and was baptized by Elder Butler K. Smith, where she has held her membership ever since. She died peacefully on the 22nd day of December at 3 o'clock p.m., aged 53 years, 10 months and 26 days.

She was a good wife, an affectionate mother and a true friend in a time of need. Her life was a life of constant toil and checkered o'er with many sorrows, yet she lived a life of faith and put her trust in Him who maketh all things work together for good of them that love God. Her last days, though filled with great bodily pain, were passed in patient waiting for the summons to come where the wicked cease to be troubled and the weary are at rest. She had no fears of death for the kind hand of the Master had parted the turbid waters of the Jordan of death, and angels on the other side beckoned her to rest, a home beyond the tide. May we, like her, be also ready."

Miller, James S.   b   d 17 Feb 1873   ? y

On the 1870 census of West River Township, Randolph County, Henry Miller was 28 and a farmer, Melissa was 25, keeping house, Mary C. was 2, and Leander W. was 1 month.

James does not appear on any census, so he was probably born sometime between the 1870 census date and his death date.

Miller, Sarah J.   b 8 May 1846   d 14 May 1861   15 y 5 m 6 d

Daughter of H.D.

Obituary, Winchester Journal, May 16, 1861:

"DIED__On Tuesday morning the 14th inst., Miss Sarah Jane Miller, aged 15 years and 5 months and 6 days. In the bloom of youth when everything was joyous and happy has passed from our little circle in the north east part of town, a lovely girl. Beloved by all, endeared to all, we deeply mourn our loss. The bereavement falls heavily upon the Father and Mother, Brothers and Sisters, to whom we would tender words of condolence and sympathy."

Monger, James K.   b 1 Mar 1844   d 2 Aug 1845   1 y 5 m 22 d

James was a son of David and Elizabeth Monger.

On the 1840 census David is head of a household with a wife and 8 children in Randolph County.

On the 1850 census they are living in Sycamore Township, Hamilton County, Ohio. David is 49 and a blacksmith, Elizabeth A. is 49, Sarah J. is 21, Henrietta S. is 13, Catharine M. is 10, Matilda M. is 8 and William C. is 26.

Monger, Margaret   b 1 Mar 1828   d 19 Mar 1848   20 y 18 d

Margaret is the first wife of William C. Monger, listed on the above census. On ancestry.com there is a family tree of the Monger family. William Clay was born in 1825. He married a second time in Hamilton, Ohio on August 1, 1850 to Eliza Munday. William's parents were David and Elizabeth Hutchinson Mongor. I did not find Margaret's maiden name so I could not research her family.

Monger, Mary A.   b 18 Mar 1822   d 5 May 1841   19 y 2 m 17 d

Mary was a daughter of David and Elizabeth Monger.

Monks, Belinda Hulitt   b ?   d before 1842   ? y

Belinda was the first wife of George W. Monks. They had one son, Charles N. Monks.

Monks, Infant   b ?   d ?   infant

Infant of George and Belinda, the baby and Belinda probably died at childbirth and are buried together.

Monks, George W.   25 Apr 1814   d 4 Apr 1865   1 y

Biography from Tucker's History of Randolph County, 1882:

"GEORGE WASHINGTON MONKS was born April 25, 1814, in Hamilton County, near Cincinnati. He received the basic education taught the pioneer children, and as a young man he taught school for two terms-first in a log cabin on the David Wysong farm, and afterward on the John Robinson farm, now (1882) known as the Kemp farm. In 1836, he moved to Winchester, and found employment in a store owned by Michael Aker, an early day merchant. It is not noted when he first started to study law. He served as clerk of Randolph County for two terms, elected to replace Charles Conway, who had retired after a service of twenty-one years. Governor Wright of Indiana appointed him as a state delegate to serve at The New York World's Fair held in 1853, and in 1854 he was elected to the State Legislature and served one term, and when he returned home he first practiced law in the office of Carey S. Goodrich and later was a partner of Judge James Brown. He was interested in the improvement of the roads and the schools in Randolph County and many other things, and held office in the local agricultural society, as well as serving with the State Board of Agriculture for a number of years.

George was twice married, first to Belinda Hulitt, and they had two children, Charles, and another son who died in infancy. After the Death of Belinda, he married Mary Ann Irvin, daughter of Robert Irvin, one of the early day settlers of this county. George was the father of seven children by this marriage, Leander J., Mary E., George W., J. Irvin, Viola, Minerva B. and Segal., Mary (Irvin) Monks died in 1864 and George almost a year later."

The following biography is from the book "Portraits and Biographical Records, Randolph County Indiana" by A. W. Bowen. This book is frequently cited and can be found at the Randolph County Historical Society Museum. The biography reads as follows:

"George W. Monks was born near Cincinnati, Ohio, April 24, 1814 and came with his parents to Randolph County, Indiana in 1820. In 1839, while still almost a boy, he was nominated by the Whig party as their candidate for clerk of Randolph County and elected by a flattering majority; in 1846 he was re-elected and served until 1853. He was a faithful and efficient officer. In 1854 the republican party in this county was organized by the coalition of the anti-slavery and free soil parties, and George W. Monks was the first republican nominee from Randolph County for a legislative office; he was elected in the fall and took a prominent and active part in the session of 1854-55. He had studied law, and after his admission to the bar, he was associated in the practice for a short time with Carey S. Goodrich, afterward entering into partnership with Judge James Brown, with whom he continued until his death. He was industrious and energetic, and while he possessed a considerable income, he had no disposition to hoard his earnings, and was unselfish in the use of his money, spending it in many ways to lighten the burden of a fellow mortal less fortunate than himself; this seemed to be his idea of the use of money, and having provided well for his family, he had no inclination to amass a fortune; and more precious to his children than gold is the warm hand clasp of many a worthy pioneer who says, 'Your father was the best friend I ever had.'

In 1843 he joined the Methodist Episcopal Church, and in all his after life he was a consistent Christian. He donated to the Methodist Episcopal society of Winchester the ground upon which the present Methodist Episcopal church is built and also the parsonage lot. In 1845 he united with the Masonic fraternity at Winchester. He was a leader in the organization of the first agricultural society of the county, and was a member of the state board of agriculture for a number of years.

He was twice married, Charles N. Monks, of this county, being a son of his first marriage. Of the second marriage there are living four children: Leander J., present judge of this circuit; George W., Minerva B., of Mankota, Minn., and J. Irvin of Watertown, Dak. After the death of his second wife in 1864, he purchased land in Minnesota, intending to remove to that state with his motherless children, but before his plans could be consummated he fell ill, and on the 4th of April, 1865, his active life closed in death.

Perhaps no man was more widely known among the pioneer citizens of Randolph County and the state than 'Wash Monks', certainly none was more honored and respected."

Monks, Mary Ann Irvin   b ?   d 18 Sep 1864   ? y

Mary was the second wife of George W. above and the daughter of Robert and Mary Irvin.

Monks, John W.   b :   d 11 Jan 1865   ? y

From Tucker History, 1882:

"John Monks was one of the early pioneers of this county, and the father of a family whose members have born a prominent part in its subsequent history. He was born in one of the great cotton manufacturing districts of England in 1775, and at an early age, learned the art of weaving. When a young man, he came to the United States and found employment in his trade. In 1820, he came to this county, locating one and a half miles south of Winchester. He had no knowledge of farming, and was ill prepared for the labors of pioneer life, and beyond an occasional job of carding wool for some of his neighbors, he found no work at his trade. His wife knew more about farming, as she had been born on a farm in Kentucky. She was Matilda Elder, born in 1787, daughter of a prominent Kentucky family. John and Matilda lived near Cincinnati, Ohio before coming to Indiana, and some of the children were born there. They had seven sons, George W., Walter S., Joseph, Richard T., John, Christopher C., William and two daughters, Margaret and Susan. John died in 1840 and Matilda in 1860, and they were buried on the farm they spent so many years on. In 1869, the stones were moved to the cemetery in Winchester, Ind. They are in very good shape for ones that old, and the dates are still clearly legible." (in 1882)

We did not find a stone for John and Matilda of the above biography, who are said to have had their stones moved from the family farm to the Old Winchester. Apparently their remains are at the old family farm, and only their stones were placed in the graveyard. We did not find either stone. Our listing is for the John whose obituary is written below. I believe him to be the son of John and Matilda and a brother to George W. and Walter Scott, both of whom are also buried in the Old Winchester.

Obituary, Winchester Journal, January 13, 1865:

"John Monks died at his residence near Harrisville, on Monday morning. The deceased was a worthy citizen and his loss will be regretted by a large circle of relatives and acquaintances. He was buried in the Winchester graveyard, by the Odd Fellows, of which Order he was a member."

Monks, Priscilla   b 1822   d 11 Jun 1861   39 y 6 m 26 d

Priscilla Kelly was married to Walter Scott Monks on September 13, 1838 in Randolph County.

Monks, Walter Scott   b 26 sep 1816   d 23 Mar 1873   56 y 9 m 27 d

A military marker was found for Walter Scott, but was in poor condition, so was replaced with a new marker during the graveyard's restoration. Now we have another mystery! Did Walter Scott, son of John and Matilda actually enlist as a private on July, 10, 1863 at the age of 46? Unable to find another Walter S., I think he did. His military record suggests that he enlisted and was discharged on the same date, but it is not very specific. Perhaps he did not have active service time. However, the Veteran's Administration did provide a military stone for him on two occasions, one when he was originally buried and a replacement stone during the restoration.

On the 1850 census of White River Township, Randolph County, Walter is 39 and a farmer, his wife is Priscilla age 29 and they have the following children: Cynthia Ann 10, Malinda 8, George W. 8 and Wright 2.

On the 1860 census Walter is a farmer, Priscilla is 39 and keeping house, and the children are: Cantha (Cynthia Ann) 20, G.W.,16, Wright, 11, Levi, 9, Sarah J., 7 and John, 3.

Priscilla died the next year (1861) and on February 5, 1867, Walter S. married Mary W. Adney in Randolph County by J. Eltzroth.

On the 1870 census, Walter is 54 and a farmer, Mary is 39, Sarah is 16, John is 14, William Adney is 16 and Catherine Adney is 10.

Obituary, Winchester Journal, March 26, 1873:

"Walter Scott Monks, residing on the Huntsville Rd., about two miles southwest of town, died on Sunday morning last, after a long and painful illness of erysipelas."

Monroe, A.D.C.   b 24 Dec 1823   d 1 May 1862   38 y 5 m 8 d

On the 1860 census of White River Township, Randolph County, A.D.C. is 36 and a carpenter, his wife Mary J. is 26 and they have children Warren W., age 10 and Zoe, age 6 months. Also living with them is Hannah Monroe, age 70, probably the mother of A.D.C.

His will was recorded in 1862 and read as follows:

" I, Alonzo D. Monroe of Winchester in the County of Randolph and State of Indiana, do make and publish this my last will and testament, First I direct that my body be decently interred and that my funeral be in a manner corresponding with my estate situation in life; and as to such worldly estate I may be possessed of, I dispose of the same in the following manner to wit:

I direct first that all my just debts and funeral expenses be paid as soon after my decease as possible, out of my portion of my estate that may come to the hands, including tomb stones for myself and family. And I give and bequeath to my beloved wife, Mary Jane, all of my estate of what solvent nature, subject to the payment of my debts, and to such provisions for my beloved son, Warren W. Monroe as to her may seem just and proper under all the circumstances. What may exist at the time of my death the amount thus determined upon to be paid over to the guardian of my son to be by him invested in Wild Lands or otherwise at the discretion of said guardian to and for the use of my said son, and in the event of the death on my son before he arrives at the age of twenty-one years and unmarried, then under that case his portion of my estate shall immediately vest in and become the property of my wife and her heirs and I hereby nominate and appoint my esteemed friend Isaac Smith of Randolph County guardian of the person and estate of my son Warren W. Monroe.

And lastly, I do hereby constitute and appoint by dearly beloved wife Mary Jane to be sole executor of this my last will and testament, revoking any and all former wills by me heretofore made and confirming this and none other to be my last will and testament. In witness whereof I alone, A.C. Monroe, the testator have here set my hand and sealed this on the 15th day of April, A.D. 1862,"

The will was witnessed by Carey S. Goodrich

Morrow, Mary Adella (Bowen)   b ?   d 13 Apr 1889   ? y

Obituary, Winchester Journal, April 14, 1880:

"DIED__In this city yesterday morning, Mrs. Mary Adella, wife of R.B. Morrow. The deceased had typhoid pneumonia and leaves a husband and three small children and many friends to mourn the loss of a kind wife, affectionate mother and true friend. The remains will be kept until the arrival of H.O. Bowen, who is en route from San Francisco and particulars of the funeral cannot yet be given."

R.B Morrow was owner of a clothing business in Winchester.

Neff, Emily Charlene   b 7 Aug 1829   d 30 Aug 1860   31 y 23 d

A marriage record was found in Randolph County, March 4, 1849, Allen O. Neff to Emily Garrett.

Emily was the daughter of Nathan Garrett and Sarah Puckett Garrett.

On the 1850 census of Winchester Allen O. is 23 and a printer and Emily is 20.

On the August 1, 1860 census of Winchester, Emily Neff, age 31, was living with Duane and Henrietta Garrett for unknown reason. It may have been that she was ill since she died August 30, same year, same month as the census was taken. Also in the same household was Sylvania Garrett, age 26, a school teacher. Duane was Emily's brother and Sylvania was her sister.

A.O. Neff enlisted in Co. G, Indiana 8th Infantry on May 9, 1861, was promoted to full 2nd lieutenant on March 5, 1863 and mustered out June 18, 1863.

On the 1870 census Emily's husband, Allen O. Neff, is 46, married to Louisa and they have 2 children, Eddie, age 2 and Eliza B., age 1.

Allen died in 1880 and was buried originally in the Old Winchester. His remains were moved to Fountain Park Cemetery, but Emily's remains were not moved.

Neff, John Sr.	b 1770	d 1855	85 y
Neff, Susan	b ?	d 1852	76 y

On the 1850 census of White River Township, Randolph County, John Neff Sr. is 78, his wife Susan is 74 and William Neff, age 41, is living with them.

Neff, Infant	b ?	d ?	? m

This is a child of John Neff Jr. and Harriett N. Holmes. No other information was found.

Chapter Twelve

William Page and the Women of Winchester

I am really happy that I have the chance to finally tell my story. My name is William Page and I was born in Kentucky. The family moved here about the mid 1830's, and I think it's been a good place for me to live, start a business, get married and raise our children. I say my main business was operating a grocery store, but others refer to my place as a groggery. (a slightly disreputable place to buy liquor) Just a couple of years before I died, I bought the Franklin House, a fine hotel at the corner of Main and Franklin, on the square. For months I applied for a liquor license and was turned down several times before it finally got approved. Before I could make the Franklin House the great place I wanted it to be, I got sick with the fever and died. Even though I was a successful businessman there were many in Winchester who looked down on me. Some of them were those nosy women who wanted to ban alcohol, the temperance women, they were called. Now I get the chance to tell you why they gave me so much trouble.

Back in 1854 I owned a grocery store and also happened to sell a little liquor on the side. I had a neighbor and friend named Thornton Alexander. Like me, Thornton was married with several children. He was respected in our town and at one time had even been the sheriff of Randolph County. But Thornton had a problem with the drink and in 1854 when this all happened he was a drunkard. He got so hard up for money to buy liquor that he started selling off the family possessions until he had sold off everything including Eliza's featherbed and cow.

The family was destitute. Out of money and liquor, he got the DT's (delirium tremens) and died on March 28, 1854. He was 45 years old.

The next thing I know his wife, Eliza, and about 80 other women came storming into my grocery, kicking and knocking things over. One by one they poured every barrel of whisky and rye, every keg and barrel of alcohol I owned; they poured every last bit of it out onto the street! One of them, Amanda Way, had a gun and I knew she could use it, so all I could do was watch the destruction. I saw one old sot lying to the ground trying to suck up that booze before the ground absorbed it.

I was sorry Thornton drank too much and died. He was my neighbor and my friend. Our wives were friends, our children played together. But just because I sold liquor, it didn't make his drinking problem my fault. I had no choice but to sue those women. Do you think I could get me a lawyer in Winchester? Not a one would represent me because all of their wives were involved in the destruction of my liquor supply.

Finally I got a lawyer from out of town and we went before Judge Silas Colgrove. The ladies were indicted for malicious trespass and the case went to jury trial. The papers called it the "Page Liquor Case" and it caused quite a stir in Winchester. Within 30 minutes of deliberation the jury found them not guilty. I couldn't believe it! I had to bring a civil suit to recover the damage and was awarded $400 to cover the cost of the liquor and the barrels and kegs they smashed. Since that incident a lot of people have been cool toward me, unfairly I might add.

Thornton is buried out here someplace. I guess we were destined to remain neighbors. Eliza got remarried and she and the children moved to Illinois with her new husband. I never did hear from any of them again.

My wife's name was Elizabeth and we had the following children: John, Nancy, Thomas, Sarah, Mary, George ,Henraetta and Willard (Willie). Henraetta died when she was four and is buried here with me. My sister, Isabella Ennis, died within a week of me and she's buried here too. My son, Willie, is also buried here.

I sure didn't expect to get ill and die so quickly but there is no way to predict one's future. I found financial and business success in Winchester and believe that I did a lot of good for Winchester, even if some temperance people wouldn't agree.

Page, Henraetta   b 15 Jan 1850   d 17 Jan 1854   4 y 2 d

Page William M.   b 24 Aug 1811   d 18 May 1865   53 y 9 m 25 d

Tucker's History of Randolph County has the following information related to William Page:

Winchester was incorporated as a town in 1838 by popular vote. (38 for, 0 against) William Page voted yes. Pg. 73

William Page was awarded a grocery bond, 1839. Pg 73

The "Page Liquor Case," detailed report, 1854. Pgs. 73, 190, 290

Page 73 is worth including in this book. Remember, Mr. Tucker wrote the book in 1882, when the temperance movement was picking up considerable steam, leading to the eighteenth amendment being ratified in 1919 .

"Thornton Alexander is probably the one who was afterward elected Sheriff, became a sot, and finally died some years afterward with delirium tremens; and from his desolate dwelling while his lifeless corpse lay stiff and gaunt therein, the ladies of Winchester, headed by the widow of the wretched man, marched in long and grim procession to the groggery of William Page and, knocking in the heads of his barrels and what-not, spilled the abominable, murderous stuff into the street, out of which startling transaction grew the noted "Page Liquor Case", so famous twenty-five years ago. And the same terrible demon of the drink traffic raises still its devilish head, and eagerly goes about to destroy everything fair and lovely and of good report. Hundreds, possibly thousands, of indictments have been effected against liquor sellers in Randolph County, and scores of men have been fined for selling strong drink "contrary to law." Yet men are to be found who, for money, will carry on the mischievous traffic, and law-makers will still play with the wild beast, alcohol, as though it were a merry, gamboling kitten to be petted and cuddled, instead of being, as it is, a fierce and ruthless monster to be throttled and slain, with its horrid carcass burned to ashes and scattered to the four winds."

1850 census of Winchester lists William M. as 41 and a grocery keeper, Elizabeth is 37, John is 9, Nancy J. is 7, Thomas S. is 5, Mary A. is 2 and Henraetta is 6 months.

On the 1860 census William is 48, Elizabeth is 45, John W. is 20, Nancy J. is 18, Thomas S. is 16, Sarah E. is 14, Mary A. is 12, George W. is 8 and Willard is 1.

The names and dates on the census, and the ages of everyone, are inconsistent. It is also confusing because there are three marriages recorded in Randolph County for Elizabeth Hester, and they are clearly three different people because each appears on succeeding census lists with families with the husband named on the marriage record, i.e. Henry D. Foust, George Sumption and William M. Page. To further confuse the writer (and probably the reader) , William M. has two marriages recorded in Randolph County, Mary Hammer in 1841 and Elizabeth Hester in 1846. I don't know what happened to Mary, but I think that John, Nancy and Thomas and maybe Sarah are from that marriage.

Death Notice, Randolph Journal, May 25, 1865:

"William M. Page, died at his residence in this place, on the morning of the 18th inst., of fever."

Page, Willard (Willie)   b 1859   d 1875   16 y

Accident Notice, Winchester paper, January 13, 1875:

"Fatal Accident-Willie Page, of this place, while riding a race horse at Celina, Ohio, last Saturday, was thrown and received injuries from which he died on Saturday morning. His remains were brought here and interred in the cemetery yesterday. The deceased was about 16 years old and had been employed at the Ross House until last week, when he left on his own account and went to Celina, where he met his death."

On the 1870 census of Winchester, Willie was age 10 and living with his sister Nancy J. Arney.

Chapter Thirteen

Melvin Parker, Civil War Soldier, Prisoner of War

My name is Melvin Parker and I am pleased to share my story with you. In 1850 I lived with my parents and brothers and sisters in Wayne County, Indiana. By 1860 we had moved to Dallas County, Iowa. I was 28 years old and a teacher. The woman I wanted to marry lived in Winchester so I returned to Indiana. In February, 1861, Sarah Brown and I were married at the residence of her parents, Thomas and Sarah E. Brown.

The Civil War was underway and I was strongly anti-slavery. I left Sarah and our newly born daughter with her family and returned to Iowa to join the 39th Iowa Infantry in August of 1862. I was 30 years old at the time.

The 39th drilled near Des Moines, Iowa until December of 1862, when the regiment was fully organized. On December 13, 1862 we started for the south. Near Trenton, Tennessee two brigades were organized to move against General Forrest. We joined up with the 50th Indiana. The battle lasted for several hours. The 39th was under heavy fire and fought bravely.

In January of 1863 our regiment moved to Corinth, Tennessee and joined with the Iowa Third Brigade and stayed in that area for several months. In April, my company, Company H, was sent a few miles from Corinth to guard a corral. We were surrounded by several hun-dred of the enemy's cavalry and our captain and most of Company H was captured, including me.

We were told that the purpose of taking us as prisoners was to allow us to live, but deprive the Union of our services. To have been killed on the battlefield would have been more humane. Our most intense battle was simply to survive until the end of the war. I will tell you about my experience as a prisoner of the confederacy. We were searched and then marched to the rear. Once behind the lines we were lined up and searched again. They took all of our possessions: knapsacks, shelter tents, overcoats, blankets, even the contents of our pockets. They also took our shoes, a serious loss since we faced a very long march. Some of my fellow prisoners even had their clothes taken. During our long march to Libby prison we were kept in community jails along the way. We would be forced to march as many as 150 miles in 6 days through rain, mud and snow. Several of our men died of exposure along the way.

Sometimes we were packed into cattle cars and taken by train packed like sardines. No one could sit and food rations and water were not provided on these trips. Those of us who survived the long anguishing trip arrived at Libby Prison during the night. We were sick, exhausted, hungry, thirsty and disoriented. Several were barely alive. We were marched like cattle, being prodded and struck from behind. When we entered the prison, we heard shouts saying "fresh fish, fresh fish." All of the prisoners gathered around us to learn what regiment we were from and the latest about the war. Most of us new prisoners were so overwhelmed by the condition of the prisoners and the smell of the compound that we began vomiting.

During my many months in confinement I spent some time in Andersonville Prison also, but most of my time was in Libby. There were usually about 4000 prisoners there. The place was filthy beyond description. Within minutes of arrival our clothes and bodies were covered with vermin. Most of the men had layers of dirt on them and their skin was in terrible condition. Before long we became as they were. Deaths occurred daily and soon we hardly noticed because each of us was fighting our own individual battle to survive.

But we prisoners did everything we could to maintain our sanity and our very lives. We had a chess club and a debating club. We also had religious groups and foreign language clubs. By late 1863 we even had a newspaper called the Libby Prison Chronicle. A chaplain from New York collected information from prisoners, prepared a single hand-written copy and read it to us. These weekly reports took our minds off our prison conditions which kept getting worse. By mid-1863 our daily rations were two ounces of meat, half a pound of bread and a small cup of beans or rice.

We were surrounded by disease, starvation and death. Most men lost all hope of being released and for many death was welcomed....better than the agony of our existence.

I wanted more than anything to return to Sarah and our baby daughter, Ella. But that dream was not to be. I died on January 23, 1864 while a prisoner at Libby. My diseased and starving body could no longer survive.

My tombstone is here in this graveyard beside that of my wife, Sarah, my father-in-law and mother-in-law, Thomas and Sarah Brown and my sister-in-law and brother-in-law, Squire and Martha Welker.

I don't really know if my bones are here or somewhere in the south, but my spirit is here with my wife and family beside me.

Parker, Melvin, Pvt.　　　　b 1832　　　d 1 Jan 1864　　　32 y

On the 1850 census of Perry Township, Wayne County, Indiana, Joseph Parker is 47 and a farmer, Margaret is 50, Ogilva is 25 and a carpenter, Pleasant is 23 and a carpenter, Sally is 19, Melvin is 18 and a laborer, Luiza is 16 and Clifford is 13.

American Civil War Soldiers records lists Melvin Parker as enlisting on August 8, 1862 at age 30 and died as a prisoner in Richmond, Virginia.

Parker,   b 20 Mar 1830   d 23 Dec 1899   69 y 9 m 3 d
Sarah E. Brown

The Civil War Pension index lists Sarah E. Parker as getting a pension from the death of Melvin Parker.

Obituary, Winchester Journal, December 29, 1899:

"PARKER-Sarah Elizabeth Parker was born in Preble County, Ohio, March 20, 1830 and died in Winchester, Ind. Dec. 23, 1899, age 69 years, nine months and three days. She was the daughter of Thomas and Sarah E. Brown, who were pioneers in Indiana having settled here from Penn. about 60 years ago. Her childhood was spent in an uneventful way with the struggles of pioneer life in a new country among poor people. She educated herself for teaching and taught 18 schools of 3 months each. She was married to Melvin J. Parker Feb. 9, 1861. Soon after their marriage her husband enlisted in the service of his country in Co. 39th Regt. Iowa Vols. He was taken prisoner while serving his country and was for a long time in Andersonville and Libby prisons. He died of starvation and disease in prison in Feb. 1864.

There was born to them as the fruits of said marriage, Dec. 8, 1861, one child, Ella M., who still survives. Sarah never remarried after the death of her husband, but took up the battle of life alone and reared and educated her daughter until she graduated in our High School and married.

The deceased joined the M.E. Church in early life and while never active in church work she continued in the faith. Her father, mother and sister, Martha Welker, were members of the Christian Church and her faith in after years more inclined to be with them though she never changed her church relations.

She was a good mother to her only daughter and a kind neighbor to the poor and needy and especially so to her father and mother while they lived, and to her sister, Martha Welker, who was for many years an invalid as was also her husband, Squire Welker. Her good deeds are best known to those to whom she ministered and will not be forgotten. She had her faults and peculiarities but with all she was benevolent and kind, and did what she could to help those under her care.

After appropriate services at the Christian Church, conducted by Eld. I.P. Watts, she was, at her own request, laid to rest beside her father, mother and sister in the family lot in the old cemetery at Winchester, Ind., to await the final resurrection."

Sarah was the last person known to have been buried in the Old Winchester Graveyard.

CHAPTER FOURTEEN

Payne, Joseph – Reece, Susannah

Payne, Joseph b ? d 26 Jan 1876 ? y

Joseph is the husband of Rebecca

Winchester Journal, July, 30, 1873:

"ACCIDENT – Joseph Payne, an old citizen of this place, fell from the mow in Mrs. Goodrich's barn yesterday and was severely injured. Dr. Bosworth was called in and after a careful examination ascertained that no bones were broken, but it is feared that he is injured internally. He was resting easier last evening and hopes are entertained that he will recover."

Apparently he did recover since he lived another 2.5 years.

Payne, Rebecca b 24 Sep 1798 d 1 Jul 1880 81 y 9 m 1 d

Obituary, Winchester paper, July 21, 1880:

"DIED__At the residence of her son-in-law, E. Corwin, in Winchester, Ind., July 1ˢᵗ A.D. 1880, aged 81 years, 9 months and 1 day. Rebecca Keener was born Sept. 24, 1798 in Knox County,

Tennessee, was united in marriage with Joseph Payne March 20, 1822, and five years later emigrated to this State with her husband who preceded her to the Spirit land Jan. 26, 1876. Mother Payne accepted Jesus as her Savior when quite young and joined the Methodist Church of which denomination her parents were members and sought to rear their children in the ways of truth and righteousness. About four years ago she united with the Society of Friends of which branch of the church militant she was a worthy member when called to her reward. Four sons and three daughters learned to call her by the endearing name of mother. They are all living and except two were present to look for the last time on the dear form of her who watched over them in infancy, shared their joys and griefs in childhood and youth and loved them to the end. They sorrow deeply for the loss of this best earthly friend but not as those without hope, having the assurance if they seek the Lord while he may be found and call upon him while he is near, they may ere long meet dear mother where sickness, sorrow and death are unknown, and while we prize the holy, pure, disinterested love of mother we should point the sorrowing ones to the source of love to the sympathizing Jesus whose love surpasses that of the most devoted earthly friend to him who alone is able to save to the utmost. May we all be wise enough to walk in the paths of righteousness for his name sake and be permitted in the sweet by and by to unite with the dear ones who today are with him in Paradise.

Mother, rest , thy sorrows o'er, Weight of care no more to feel

Thought we meet on earth no more, Jesus can our sorrows heal.

Brothers sisters, hear him calling, from the beauteous golden strand

Calling gently, calling to us, Meet Mother in the better land."

Payne, Elizabeth   b ?   d 22 Feb 1885   46 y ?

Obituary, Winchester Journal, February 25, 1885:

> "The wife of Thomas Payne, died of consumption last Sunday morning. Her remains were interred at the old cemetery. The deceased was a daughter of Michael Hobbich, and was a most estimable lady."

Pettee, Amanda Jane   b 25 Mar 1848   10 Nov 1871   23 y 7 m 16 d

Amanda was the wife of C.L. Pettee, according to her tombstone.

Obituary, Winchester Journal, Nov, 1871:

> "Died at the residence of T.F. Colgrove, in Winchester, Indiana, Mrs. JANE AMANDA PETTEE, daughter of Ephriam and Hannah Adams. Mrs. Pettee was born March 26th, 1848 in Jasper, Steuben County, N.Y. and removed to the State of Indiana with her parents at the age of six years where she resided until 1850, when she removed to Wellington, Ohio.
>
> At the time of her death, she was on a visit with friends and relatives at Winchester. Wednesday night at a late hour she retired in usual health and spirits, apparently. About half past 1 o'clock Thursday morning she gave the alarm, and when a light was produced she was found in a fainting condition and her clothing and the floor were covered with blood, the result of a Gastric Ulcer in the stomach. Thursday night and Friday morning she continued to vomit blood in great quantities, and at 11:30 o'clock A.M., Friday, notwithstanding the best of medical attendance and the care of anxious friends, she died.

The funeral sermon was preached by Rev. W.F. Walker at the M.E. church, after which the remains were placed in the Winchester cemetery. Mrs. Pettee was a kind and loving companion, and an exemplary wife and mother. She leaves a husband and one child, with numerous friends to mourn her sudden death."

Philips, Evaline (Way)   b 3 Jul 1839   d 19 Feb 1872   33 y

On the 1850 census of Winchester, Jesse Way is 42, Lucinda Way is 38 and the following reside in the home with them: Eliza Hamwood, age 21, Sarah J. Manger, age 20, Henry Way, age 14, Evaline Way ,age 11, Caroline Way, age 9, William R. Way ,age 7, Thos. J. Way, age 5 and Mary A.E. Way, age 3.

On the 1870 census of Franklin Township, Randolph County, Albert Philips is 38, Evaline is 31 and they have one child, Frances, age 10.

Obituary, Winchester Journal, February 21, 1872:

"DIED__ On Monday last at the residence of her husband, Mr. Albert Philips, daughter of Mr. and Mrs. Jesse Way of this city. The remains will be interred in the cemetery in the city today."

For those who have Quaker history interests, there is a genealogy book on the Way family at the Randolph County Historical Society Museum. It states the following about Jesse Way on page 84:

"Jesse Way came to Indiana from South Carolina as a boy of seven, with his parents and other Friends who were making the pioneer move to a new and natural wilderness where land could be secured. "

Jesse was a Friend (Quaker) as shown by White River MM minutes. Also in the minutes 4 July 1829,

" Jesse Way left at liberty to marry Fanny Diggs. 1 Aug 1829, reported marriage accomplished. " (This marriage was approved by the Quaker Church.)

22 Sept 1834,

"Jesse Way, of Dunkirk, complained for marrying contrary to discipline." (Jesse was a widower who married outside the Quaker faith.)

17 Nov 1834,

" disowned."

The information further states that Fanny Diggs, the daughter of William and Fanny (Crews) Diggs, died 15 Jan, 1832 in Winchester. Jesse married Lucinda Turner, daughter of Randolph and Elizabeth (Heaston) Turner on 28 Jun 1834. The book also states

"In Lucinda's obituary it states she came to Winchester in Nov. 1833, with her mother and two brothers; was a member of the Presbyterian, formerly a Friend."

Jesse and Fanny had one child, Susannah. Jesse and Lucinda had John H., Henry T., Mary C., Eveline W., Caroline W., William Randolph, Thomas J., Mary Ann Elizabeth, Phebe L., Hulda Alice and James Liston.

Jesse Way was at various times a farmer, merchant or businessman of Winchester. He was at one time a clerk and for three years was a member of the Board of Directors of the State Bank of Indiana.

Porter, Oscar   b 1858   d 23 Dec 1881   23 y

Oscar was the son of Robert Porter and Elmira Way Porter. Elmira was the daughter of Solomon and Catherine Way. Oscar was the nephew of Amanda Way, known for her participation in the temperance movement.

On the 1860 census of White River Township, Randolph County, Hannah Way was 57, her daughter, Amanda, was 21, Robert Porter was 28 and a cabinet maker, Elmira Porter was 20 and Oscar was 2.

I found no other information about the Porter family.

Prather, Clifford H.   b 1870   d 5 Jul 1870   4 m

Obituary, Winchester Journal, July 7, 1870:

> "DIED__In this city on Tuesday evening, July 5th, 1870, CLIFFORD H., infant son of Col. And Mrs. A. W. Prather, aged about 4 months. The bereaved parents have the sympathy of the community."

Allen W. Prather and Hannah M. Linton were married in Barthalomew County, Indiana on May 27, 1861.

On the 1870 census of Winchester, Allen W. is 32 and a lawyer, Hannah is 32, Allen L. is 6, Jessie M. is 4, Kathie E. is 2, and Clifford H. is 3 months. Lazza Warren age 19 is a housekeeper.

Puckett, Baby   b 1873   d Aug 1873   4 m

Obituary, Winchester Journal, Aug. 13, 1873:

"The little 4 months old baby of Will Puckett, died on Saturday last, of Spinal Fever, after an illness of only one day. It was buried on Sunday. The afflicted parents have the sympathy of many friends."

Baby Puckett's father was William Y. Puckett. The following is from Bowen's previously cited book:

"William Y. Puckett, son of Dr. Benjamin and Mrs. Sarah (McNees) Puckett and a younger brother of Luther G., was born in Winchester, where the Randolph County bank now stands, February 23, 1843. At the age of twenty-one, he began business on his own account at teaming. In 1863, however, he enlisted in company F, One Hundred and Thirty-fourth Indiana volunteer infantry, for three months, and was honorably discharged at the expiration of the term. Subsequently after a long stay at home he enlisted in company K, One Hundred and Fifty-fourth infantry. Mr. Puckett was first married in 1872 to Belinda Monks, a native of Randolph county, and a daughter of Scott Monks, and to this union were born two children-Benjamin and Edward (plus Baby Puckett).

Mrs. Puckett was taken away August 11, 1883, and went to rest in the faith of the Methodist Episcopal church. In 1885 Mr. Puckett was married to Miss Sarah Green, a daughter of William Green, a native of White River township; and this marriage has been blessed with one child-Bernice E. In politics Mr. Puckett is a republican, and has twice been elected councilman-in 1891, 1895-being a member of the first council after Winchester was incorporated a city. Mr. Puckett has been a very industrious man, and has amassed considerable wealth, owning sixty-one acres of land, which he purchased in 1888, and four houses and lots in the city of Winchester. He is a member of the G.A.R.; and Improved Order of Red Men. He takes a great interest in the affairs pertaining to the best welfare of Winchester."

Puckett, Bennie   b 1882   d 14 Aug 1884   2 y

Son of Luther G. and Martha E.

Winchester Journal, August 20, 1884:

"Little Bennie, the two year old babe of L.G. Puckett, died last Thursday night. The little fellow had been afflicted all his life, and death was a relief to his poor suffering body. The family have the sympathy of many friends."

Puckett, Clyde (also spelled Clide)
          b 1880   d 27 Aug 1882   2 y 6 m 23 d

Son of Luther G., and Martha E.

Puckett, Mary   b ?   d ?   ? y

Daughter of Luther G., and Martha E.

Puckett, Maggie   b ?   d ?   ? y

Daughter of Luther G., and Martha E.

The following information about Luther G. is from Bowen's previously cited book:

"Luther G. Puckett, a highly respected resident of Winchester, was born in White River township, April 9, 1838, and is a son of Dr. Benjamin and Sarah (McNees) Puckett, the former of whom was a practicing physician in the township for forty-seven years. The parents died respectively in 1871, and 1849, and of their four children, two are still living in Winchester, Luther G. and William Y. The parents were members of the Society of Friends and in politics, the father was a republican.

Luther G. Puckett made his home with his father until thirty years of age. He studied dentistry with Dr. I.M.Ross, of Winchester for three years and then, for two and a half years was a partner with his preceptor, since when he has been in business on his sole account. On August 13, 1862, Mr. Puckett enlisted for three years in company H., Eighty-fourth Indiana volunteer infantry, and bravely served until June 14, 1865, when he was honorably discharged, the war having ended. During his service he participated in the battles of Shelbyville, Tenn., Lookout Mountain, Chickamauga, Missionary Ridge, Buzzard's Roost, Resaca, Altoona, Kenesaw Mountain, Atlanta, Jonesboro Lovejoy, Franklin, Nashville, and several other regular engagements, besides numerous skirmishes and raids.

On his return to Randolph county, he engaged in the grocery and bakery business, in conjunction in a limited way, with dentistry and carried on these until 1893, when he sold out and retired, receiving a pension of $12 per month for injuries received while in the service.

The marriage of Mr. Puckett took place January 3, 1871, in Shelby county, Ohio, to Martha Ellen Lovett, a native of that county, born December 8, 1849. Her parents were Owen and Mary J. (Richardson) Lovett, the former of whom was a native of

Pennsylvania and the latter a native of Ohio, where she died in 1853. The father died in Indiana.

The children born to Luther G. Puckett and wife numbered seven, named as follows: Robert B., Oak, Clyde deceased, Mary deceased, Maggie M. deceased, Bennie, deceased, and Margaret E. Mr. Puckett is a republican and has filled the office of town councilman two terms. He is a Knight of Honor, a member of Mohawk tribe, No. 72, I.O.R.M. and of the G.A.R. Mrs. Puckett is a member of the Relief Corps, G.A.R., and is also a member of Pocahontas, Nokomis Council, No. 6, I.O.R.M."

Puckett, Welcome   b 1801   d 4 Nov 1854   53 y 21 d

Welcome was the son of Joseph and Mary Puckett and the husband of Juliana Garrett, whom he married December 30, 1839 in Randolph County.

On the 1850 census W.G. Puckett is 38 and Juliana is 35. They have no children listed.

In Welcome's will signed July 16, 1849, he leaves everything to his wife, Juliana, and also names her his executrix. No children are listed.

I do not know when Juliana died or where she is buried.

Pullen, Oren E.   b ?   d ?   ? y

On his stone his parents are listed as J. and M. Only the top half of his tombstone was found so there are no dates. I was unable to find any information about this child or his parents.

Ramsey, David B.   b 17 Oct 1802   d 6 Sep 1864   62 y

David was the husband of Mary A. Favorite.

On the 1860 census of White River Township, Randolph County, David is 57 and a farmer, Mary A. is 37 and they have three children listed, Henry F., 18, James A., 16 and Martin R., 14.

In David's will he left his land and possessions to his wife, and upon her death to his three sons. Mary died in 1883. I don't know where she is buried but she is not listed in Fountain Park, so likely her remains are with her husband in the Old Winchester Graveyard.

Ramsey, James   fragment of stone only, no dates readable

Ramsey, Maria   b 1781   d 2 Feb 1852   71 y

On her tombstone it says she was the wife of James. It is probable that James and Maria were the parents of David B. above. According to a family history I found on ancestry.com, David B. had a father named Samuel James Ramsey and a mother named Mariah.

Reece, Susannah   b 10 Apr 1776   d 31 May 1850   74 y

I was not able to find any information about Susannah. She was born in 1776, the year of our country's Declaration of Independence. What changes she saw in her 74 years.

Chapter Fifteen

The Nathan Reed Family

Reed, Anna   b 1808   d 25 Mar 1872   64 y

Anna was the first wife of Nathan Reed and the mother of his children. She was the daughter of Paul and Achsah Way.

On the 1850 census of White River Township, Randolph County, Nathan is 38, Ann is 42, Caroline is 15, James Estep is 10, Eveline is 8, Emily is 6, Erastus is 4 and William W. is 2.

Reed, Erastus H.   b 10 ? 1845   d 20 Aug 1864   18 y 10 m

Obituary, Winchester newspaper, August, 1864:

> "Erastus Reed, aged about 19 years, son of Nathan and Ann Reed, died in Hospital at Madison, Indiana of the 20th inst., of black jaundice after a very short illness. He was a member of the 134th Reg., Co. F, Indiana Vols. He was brought home on Monday night and interred on Tuesday at 1 o'clock p.m. This is indeed a sad and severe affliction. The father is far away in the west. Every time that we heard from the deceased the news was that he was remarkably healthy and robust and a model soldier. Another sacrifice to this mean, and unprovoked, slave holding rebellion."

Reed, James E.   b 1840   d 17 May 1857   17 y 6 m 16 d

Article, Winchester newspaper, May, 1857:

"Sad and Fatal Accident: It becomes our painful duty this week to record a most unfortunate and distressing affair, which occurred near this place on Saturday afternoon last, and which resulted in the death of the eldest son of Mr. Nathan Reed, deputy Sheriff of this county. The circumstances attending the sad occurrence are, as near as we have been able to gather them, about as follows: Jas. Estep Reed, a lad between 16 and 17 years of age who was learning the trade of a saddler under Mr. Thos. L Scott, of this place, started in company with Harman Wager, who is also an apprentice to the same gentleman, on a hunting excursion. Before leaving town, however, the two young men were joined by William Manderbach, a baker in the employ of Mr. Binager, and the party proceeded together to the woods. Having hunted some time and finding little or no game, they concluded to amuse themselves awhile in shooting at a mark. A suitable place was accordingly selected, a target prepared, and the shooting commenced.

Young Reed, having discharged his rifle, went to examine the target, and was returning to where his comrades were standing. He had advanced to within a few steps of Wager who, it seems, was in the act of raising his gun to fire, when, by some unaccountable accident, the gun was discharged, and its contents were lodged in the body of young Reed-the ball entering the left side of the abdomen and lodging near the right side of the back.

The unfortunate young man immediately threw up his hands exclaiming 'Boys, I am shot!'. They, however, thinking he was jesting, treated the matter accordingly; and not until he advanced a step or two, and, becoming sick and faint, had laid himself down upon the ground, did the startling truth of his remark reveal itself to them. Upon ascertaining the condition of their comrade, the two young men became at once exceedingly alarmed and excited, and for some moments were undetermined how to act. Finally Wager, who refused to leave his young friend Reed for a single moment, sent Manderbach for assistance which he soon procured, and Reed was carried to the nearest house, and from thence he was conveyed in a wagon to his father's residence, between one and two miles from where the accident occurred.

His sufferings were intense, yet he bore them manfully and with scarcely a murmur. He retained his reason up to within a few moments of his decease, and gave repeated assurances of a perfect resignation to the will of an All-wise Providence. He lingered in great pain for nearly twenty-four hours, when he was released by death from his sufferings. His remains were interred on Monday last, according to the rights and ceremonies of the I.O Good Templars-of which Order he was a member-and were followed to the grave by an immense concourse of our citizens. An able and deeply impressive funeral discourse was delivered at the M.E. Church by Rev. Mr. Gillum."

Nathan Reed, husband of Anna and father of Erastus and James E., was one of Winchester's earliest pioneers. When he died his obituary was quite long; but because it contains so much history of the area I am including it in its entirety.

"Nathan Reed is Gone: Such were the sad words that came from the room where he had suffered so long and severely, at 10 o'clock last Thursday. While his death was not unexpected, yet the announcement was a shock to all. Few men have filled so large or important a part in the history of our county during the past fifty-eight years. He is the last one of the old-time officials of this county, and he leaves an official as well as a private life on which there is not a stain or blemish. He had reached a ripe old age, and was a well-preserved man, seemingly with several years of life before him, when he met with an accident that resulted in his death.

It was on the evening of Tuesday , October 18, last, that he went out on the verandah, at his residence, before retiring for the night, and miscalculating where he was stepped off, breaking the neck of his right thigh bone. From the very first he seemed to anticipate the result, and stated to the friends who were assisting him to bed, that it was the last of him. As an instance of his excellent physical condition, the night before he was injured, he rode with Hon. A.J. Stakebake, in his buggy, to Losantville and returned home. When he proposed to his friend Stakebake to go with him, the latter said to him that he would be glad to have him go, but he feared the trip would be too much for him. Mr. Reed promptly responded, 'I can stand it as well as you can, and I want to go and hear you make the speech.' He went and enjoyed it ever so much. When we take into consideration that the distance traveled in going and coming was thirty-eight miles, it shows that he was a vigorous man for one of his years.

Nathan Reed was born in Fayette County, Penn., June 7, 1813, and was therefore, seventy-nine years, seven months and nineteen days old.

He spent his boyhood days in that county, working on his father's farm during the summer months, and attending the common schools during the winter, acquiring a good education for those early days. He had heard and read of the great West, and of the opportunities offered young men that he could not hope to receive at his old home, and early in life he resolved to come West. Soon after becoming of age, in the early part of the year 1835, he bade farewell to parents, relatives and friends, and the scenes of his childhood and headed to Indiana which was then considered the 'Great West'. He came to Winchester and located, and continued to reside, in and near this city during the remainder of his life. He at once secured employment with Paul W. Way, who was then keeping a hotel here, remaining in his employ nine months, receiving $75 for his service, which was considered good pay in those early days.

After leaving Mr. Way he was engaged in various employments, saving a little money each year, steadily meeting with the success he aspired to. In the year 1839 he was appointed Constable, and soon afterward as Deputy Sheriff of the County. He served as Deputy under the administration of the different Sheriffs until August 28, 1844, when he entered upon the duties of Sheriff himself. He served until September 6, 1846, being appointed to fill a vacancy caused by the man who had been elected to that position refusing to serve. In 1846 he was elected Sheriff on the Whig ticket, receiving a larger majority than any other candidate on the ticket as was shown in these columns two weeks ago, the figures being taken from the ticket of that year, found among the papers of the late Thos. Ward. He entered upon his second term September, 6, 1846 and served until August 28, 1848. He subsequently served as Deputy Sheriff under the succeeding Sheriffs until the death of Sheriff Jenkins who died during his term of office and was not connected with that office any more.

He was the first Trustee of this township under the new Constitution serving one term as such.

He had full faith in the growth and prosperity of our county and invested his earnings in real estate near this place. He owned what is known as the Elisha Martin farm, on the Bundy Pike, which he improved and developed, selling it at a very handsome advance over what he paid for it. He subsequently owned the Obediah Fields farm, two miles west of town on the Windsor Pike, and realized a good profit on its purchase and sale. He has owned several other valuable farms in different parts of the county, all of which he had sold, except the farm in Washington Township, so long occupied by his s N. Monks, which goes to his daughter, Mrs. Monks. He owned the old Journal corner Block, and the Hardware Building on the west side of the Square at the time of his death, both of which were good investments, and brought him a very nice income.

He served as Count Commissioner from the December Term, 1865, to the December Term, 1866, filling that responsible position to the satisfaction of all. In 1871, he was elected Justice of the Peace, of this Township, to fill the vacancy caused by the death of Jacob Eltzroth, and served two years, when he was re-elected, and served four years more. He was elected to a third term in 1877, and resigned June 10, 1879, on account of the office interfering with other duties.

At the organization of the Farmers' and Merchants' Bank in April, 1878, he was elected one of its Directors. At the organization of the Board, he was elected President, and was reelected to that position each succeeding year until April, 1892, when he declined reelection, intending to spend his remaining years in ease, as his long and active life most certainly entitled him to do.

While he retired from the Presidency, he did not leave the Bank, but was a Director until his death and when at home was at the Bank a portion of almost every business day until the sad accident occurred that confined him to his bed until released by death.

He was married in 1836 to Miss Annie Way, daughter of his first employer here, Paul W. Way, with whom he lived happily until she was removed from his side by death in March, 1872. They were the parents of six children, three sons and three daughters, all of whom arrived at the age of man and womanhood. One son died in the army, another was accidentally shot and killed, and one daughter, the wife of Willliam Jarrett, passed over the River before their parents, leaving one son W.W. Reed and two daughters, Mrs. Charles Monks of Washington Township and Mrs. Perry Wysong, of Mankato, Minn., all of whom were at his bedside to mourn the loss of a most kind and indulgent father.

He was married to his present bereaved widow, who was then Mrs. Phebe Bailey, in 1873, and their married life has been one of mutual happiness and enjoyment. Their home in this city being comfortable and commodious, their many friends were always glad to meet with them and enjoy their hospitality, which was unlimited.

He joined Winchester Lodge No. 121 I.O.O.F. in the year 1857 and was a faithful and consistent member until death. He passed the chairs and represented the lodge in the Grand Lodge of the State in 1871. He was a devoted member of the Order fully believing in its great doctrines of the Universality of God and the Brotherhood of Man.

The funeral services at his residence, Sunday, were brief and simple; Rev Elkanah Beard reading part of the first verse of 5th

Chapter Second Corinthians. The choir sang a few very appropriate hymns, and Simpson Hinshaw read a brief history of the life of the deceased. The remains were taken charge of by his brethren of the I.O.O.F. and taken to the Fountain Park Cemetery where they were laid away, with the beautiful and impressive funeral service of the Order. There was a very large attendance of the Order, all the adjoining Lodges being largely represented.

This was the last sad scene in the history of the deceased; and yet we cannot close without a tribute to the memory of our departed friend. In all his positions in life, he was true to himself and true to others-we do not believe that he ever committed a wrong against anyone; he was strictly honest in all his dealing; he wanted all that was justly due to him, and he always readily and cheerfully paid unto others what was their just dues. He came to Winchester unknown and almost penniless. He accepted a humble position, as hostler and errand boy at a hotel-he did his work well, and saved the money that he earned. His sterling qualities attracted the attention of the people and by them he was honored with every position he aspired to. There is a lesson in his life for every young man in our county, and we trust they will profit by it.

In his career as Sheriff and Deputy Sheriff, he dealt with and arrested many noted and desperate criminals. He made no fuss about it, but when he was ordered to arrest violators of the law he did so fearlessly, and when he got hold of one of them, he held him until he was released by order of Court or safely landed inside of the walls of the State Prison at Jeffersonville. He ran many risks and underwent many hardships, but he always came out ahead because he was always right.

In politics, in his early life, he was a Whig; and at the death of that party, he became a Republican, and one of his greatest regrets at the accident that befell him, was that it deprived him of the pleasure of voting for the reelection of President Harrison. He was opposed to slavery and many a poor colored man fleeing from his cruel taskmaster, found in him a friend, and was sent rejoicing on his way to freedom.

In religious matters he believed in the universal salvation of all men, and that all men should do right because it was right to do right, and his life was above reproach; and with all due reverence, we assert our belief, that if all men would live the straight forward honest lives that Nathan Reed lived, there would be no need for any place for future punishment.

Among those from a distance who attended the funeral of the late Nathan Reed were William Way and Paul Woody, of Champaign, Ill.; Edward S. and John Fisher, Ogden, Ill.; Mr. and Mrs. I.C. Doan, Mrs. Allen and Mrs. Lydia Cook, of Richmond; Reed Alva and Ulyssus McIntire, Dayton, Ohio; Mrs. Jackson and daughter, Charles Pierce, wife and son, Mrs. E.J. Cottom, Mrs. Rose Fisher and son Clifford, Finley Ruby, and Henry D. Grahs, of Union City; S.K Hagans and Carl O'Harra, Chicago, and Albert O'Harra, Muncie."

Nathan's first wife, Anna, and his children, may or may not be buried in the Old Winchester Graveyard. Her marker, shared by their two sons and daughter, is a four-sided obelisk tall and easy to find in the graveyard. Anna is named on one side, Emily on the second side, James E. on the third side, and Erastus H. is listed on the fourth side. They also have an almost identical marker located in the Fountain Park Cemetery. While there is no documentation that their remains were moved, they are listed as part of 29 persons buried in a Reed plot. Two of those are named Baldwin and Bailey, the two deceased husbands of Phebe, Nathan's second wife. They were also originally buried in the Old Winchester Graveyard. Like others mentioned before, we respect both burial sites, uncertain where their remains are located.

We may believe that pre-nuptial agreements are only from modern times. I found it interesting that Nathan's will contained the following statement: "In view of the fact that I am carrying a large sum of life insurance for the use and benefit of my beloved wife and having a mutual anti-nuptial contract with her in relation to our respective estates, my bequest to her will not be very large......" When they married they were older, and he was a widower and she had been widowed twice. The will was written in 1893.

While doing the research for this book I had the pleasure of meeting Miss Mariana Reed, who was age 90 when I met her in 2006. Nathan and Anna Reed were her great-grandparents. Mariana resides in a retirement community in northeastern Indiana and I went there to meet her and learn some family history. She was and continues to be a delightful, bright and energetic lady, who at age 97 is still going strong! She told me that she will be the last burial in the Reed family burial plot at Fountain Park Cemetery. I am very grateful for her information and insights.

CHAPTER SIXTEEN

REINHEIMER, ELIZABETH F. –
VORIS, MICHAEL P., 2ND LT.

Reinheimer, Elizabeth F.   b 1860   d 9 Oct 1871   11 y 1 m 11 d

Winchester Journal, October 11, 1871:

> DIED___In this city on Monday last of typhoid fever, Elizabeth
> Florence, daughter of Peter Reinheimer, aged 11 years, 1 month
> and 11 days."

On the 1870 census of Winchester, Peter was 55 and a landlord (on previous census reports he was listed as a stable keeper), Elizabeth (Irvin)
was 46, Peter M. was 22 and a clerk in a grocery, Lewis A. was 15, Oliver
F. was 12, Elizabeth F. was 9, Mary E. was 7 and Lincoln was 4.

Richards, Joseph   b 1860   d 13 Apr 1872   12 y

Winchester Journal, April 17, 1872:

> "Our old friend Richards lost his son, Joseph, by death, on Sunday
> morning last. The little fellow had the measles, and when just
> recovering from them, suffered an attack of Lung Fever. He was
> sick for some time and suffered severely."

On the 1870 census of Winchester, Jacob Richards was 55, Sarah was 41, Jacob was 10, Ida was 8 and Joseph was 7. (Once again the ages do not add up, but that is what is listed on the census report. Joseph may have been 9 instead of 12 when he died.)

Romaser, Andrew   b 1807   d 16 Nov 1850   43 y

Andrew is listed on the Passenger and Immigration Lists Index as a primary immigrant 1843-1845.

On the 1850 census of White River Township, Randolph County, Andrew is 43, a teamster, born in Germany, Elizabeth is 31, also born in Germany, Mary is 12 born in Ohio, and Lucinda is 10, John is 8, Lydia A. is 6, Elizabeth is 4 and George W. is 2, all born in Indiana.

Romiser, Catherine   b 1851   d 11 Jul 1851   4 m 19 d

Catherine was a daughter of Andrew and Elizabeth. Elizabeth must have been a couple of months pregnant when Andrew died of unknown cause in 1850.

Romiser, George W.   b 1849   d 20 May 1853 4 y 4 m 3 d

George was a son of Andrew and Elizabeth.

The above three people are from one family. The name is spelled Ramaser and Romiser on gravestones and census records.

Routh, Gertrude   b 22 May 1857   d 11 Jun 1858   1 y 1 m 10 d

On Gertrude's tombstone it lists her parents as J.T.B. and E. J. I found a J.B. Routh in Winchester on both the 1860 and 1870 census reports, but not with a wife whose initials are E.J.

Routh, Sarah Elizabeth   b 1836   d 10 Feb 1859   23 y 19 d

Winchester Journal, February 17, 1859:

"On the 10th inst., after a very short illness, Mrs. Sarah Elizabeth Routh, wife of John B. Routh, aged 23 years."

Article, Winchester Journal, June 30, 1870:

"CHLOROFORMED: An attempt was made to burglarize John B. Routh's residence on Saturday night last. Chloroform was administered to Mr. Routh and his lady, but they were aroused and raised an alarm before getting entirely under its influence. It being early in the night-about 11 o'clock- several of the neighbors had not retired and came to their assistance immediately. Two of the would be burglars were seen, but in the confusion made their escape by the back way. Several of our neighboring towns have been raided by these sneak thieves, and Winchester will doubt-less receive their attention. Our citizens should be prepared to give them a warm reception."

Routh, Vianna   b 18 May 1855   d 14 Apr 1856   11 m 26 d

On Vianna's tombstone it says she was the daughter of J.T.B. and E.J.

Scott, Helen   b ?   d ?   ? y

Her tombstone says she is the daughter of T.L and L.M. There were no dates on her stone. I did not find anyone named Scott with those initials.

Segraves, Miss Jane   b ?   d 31 Oct 1872   69 y

Obituary, Winchester Journal, November, 1872:

"DIED__In this city on Thursday last, MISS JANE SEGRAVES, aged about 69 years. The deceased has resided in this city for many years. She was an industrious and quiet lady, and but few knew of her illness until her death was announced. Funeral services were held at the M.E. Church, Rev. R.D. Spellman officiating, after which the remains were interred in the cemetery."

Seagraves, Martin b 24 Mar 1808 d 11 Jan 1875 67 y

This name was also found to be spelled Segrove and Segraves on records.

On the 1850 census of White River Township, Randolph County, Martin was 43 and a shoemaker, Elizabeth was 41, Martha J. was 10, James M. was 8, Sarah E. was 6 and Anna was 4. In the same residence are listed William Addington , 43 and Elizabeth Addington, 8.

Obituary, Winchester Journal, January 20, 1875:

"Martin A. Segraves, whose death we announced last week, was born in Guilford County, North Carolina, March 24, 1808. He came to Indiana in the fall of 1829, and settled near Richmond, where he resided nearly ten years, removing at the expiration of that time to our town, where he resided until his death. He was a quiet, industrious and unobtrusive man, strictly honest in all his dealings with his fellow men. He leaves a wife and several children, relatives and friends to mourn his death."

Segraves, Telitha K. b ? Aug 1843 d 30 Apr 1860 16 y 8 m 23 d

Obituary, Winchester newspaper:

" DIED__In Winchester, Ind., on Monday, April 30, 1860, Miss Telitha K. Segraves, eldest daughter of Michael and Martha Segraves, aged 16 years, 8 months and 23 days. To know why one so young is thus removed from a large circle of friends and acquaintances, which she charmed by her cheerfulness and many amiable traits, must ever remain a mystery to us in this life. She was one whose friendship was sincere, and whose conversation was refined, affable and cordial. To her bereaved parents she was not only an obedient daughter, but a counselor and friend. Her illness was protracted and severe, yet she bore her sufferings firmly and with patience until her dissolution came, when calmly and without a struggle, the fluttering life breath left her."

On the 1870 census of Winchester, Michael Segroves is 54, Martha is 45 and they have the following children: John, age 19, Sarah E., age 16, Bell, age 11 and Frank, age 9.

Michael Segraves and Martha Wilson married in Randolph County July 26, 1842, so Telitha would have been their oldest child.

Simpson, Susanna   b 1786   d 30 Aug 1853   69 y 3 m

Her tombstone says she was the wife of Alex. No other information was found.

Smith, Cordelia S.   b ?   d ? ? 185?   22 y

Only a fragment of Cordelia's tombstone was found. On the stone she was said to be the daughter of C.A. and M.A. No information was found on this family.

Smith, Edward   b 22 Mar 1863   d 10 Dec 1870   7 y 11 m 19 d

William W. Smith and Louisa Eltzroth married November 8, 1840 in Randolph County.

On the 1870 census of Winchester, William was 55 and a farmer, Louisa was 45, John was 22, George was 15, Oliver was 8, Edward was 6 and Nellie was 4.

Obituary, Winchester Journal, December 14, 1870:

"DIED__In this city on Saturday, December 10th, 1870 of heart disease, after an illness of ten days, Edward Smith, son of William W. and Louisa Smith, age 7 years, 11 months and 19 days."

Smith, Oliver P. "Coon"   b ?   d 20 Nov 1889   29 y

Oliver was a son of William W. and Louisa.

Obituary, Winchester Journal, November 20, 1889:

"Oliver P. Smith, better known as "Coon" died Monday afternoon at 3:30 o'clock. He has been a long sufferer from consumption but never gave up until the last. His funeral took place yesterday afternoon at his father's residence, services conducted by Rev. J.B. Fowler, after which his remains were interred in the old cemetery."

On the 1880 census of Winchester, Oliver was 20 and listed as a boarder at the home of W.A. O'Harra, a blacksmith.

Snyder, Catherine   b 31 Aug 1836   d 18 Jan 1879   42 y 6 m 19 d

On the 1860 census of Winchester, George W. is 31, Catherine is 24, Anna is 6, L.J. is 4 and Fredrick is 3.

Catherine wrote a will dated November 6, 1878, leaving to Cleone L Snyder, her youngest daughter,

" my gold watch and chain, my organ which I now have in the house, my sewing machine, two beds and beddings, one bureau, washstand, portfolio, the rag carpet now in the front room and all the pictures in the house and my set of jewelry."

She also left equal amounts of money to each of the children mentioned above in the census plus two others born sometime after the 1870 census. I do not know what happened to her husband, George, but he may also be buried in the Old Winchester.

Spencer, George E.   b 5 Aug 1853   d 28 Dec 1853   7 m 21 d

George was a son of Jonas and Maria A. Smith.

On the 1860 census of White River Township, Randolph County, Jonas Spencer was 49 and a gemsmith, Maria A. was 32, Elihu 12, Thomas J. 10 and Elizabeth 8. The family moved on to Iowa where Jonas died in 1868. Thomas and Elizabeth were both living with their mother, Maria, in 1870 in Jasper, Iowa.

Summers, Henry   b 15 Jul 1784   d 10 Aug 1871   87 y 26 d

Henry was born in Augusta, Virginia, the son of Johannes John Summers (1737-1803) and Elizabeth Reidmauer (1752-1832). He married Julia Ann King November 26, 1827 in Virginia.

Obituary, Winchester Journal:

> "DIED__Henry Summers, an old citizen of this county, died at his residence in this place on Friday last. Mr. S. had been afflicted for many years, but his death was rather sudden. He was 87 years of age."

Julia Ann died some time before 1860 and is probably also buried in the Old Winchester, although no stone was found for her.

On the 1860 census of White River Township, Randolph County, Henry is 76 and his wife, Margaret is 60, so he had remarried by this census. They are both still alive on the 1870 census.

Summers, Susanna   b 1836   d 23 Jun 1853   16 y 9 m 9 d

Susanna was a daughter of Henry and Julia Ann Summers.

Teal, Dr. Asbury F.   b ?   d 5 Oct 1863   39 y

I found a marriage record for Asbury F. Teal to Mary E.S.M. White on September 19, 1859.

Death Notice, Winchester newspaper, Oct, 1863:

> "Teal, Oct. 5, 1863, Dr. A.F Teal, aged 39."

Teal, Lillie Bell W.   b 1862   d 18 Jan 1863   6 m 5 d

Her stone says she was the only child of Dr. A. F. and L.W.

I was not able to find any information on this family and am unable to say why Lillie's mother's initials on her tombstone are L.W. Lillie has a beautiful marker with both a head and footstone.

Towne, Nicholas J.   b 1790   d 26 Oct 1876   86 y

Nicholas was a soldier in the War of 1812.

On the 1850 census of Eaton, Preble County, Ohio, N.J. Town (note different spelling on this census) is 60, Susan is 54, Thomas is 20, Charles is 19, Lydia is 15 and Mary is 16. It is somewhat confusing on the 1860 census, Preble County, Ohio, when Nicholas is listed as 69 and a cooper, Susan is 26 (?), Thomas is 28 and a shoemaker, and Charles is 22 and a day laborer. The ages on the two census reports do not match but the names do.

On the 1870 census of Winchester, Nicholas is listed as 80 and a retired cooper and Susan is 40. On the 1880 census Susan is 50 and a cook in the home of W. C .Brown. It is probable that Nicholas had both a wife and a daughter named Susan and that his wife died between 1850 and 1860 in Ohio.

Obituary, Winchester Journal, November 1, 1876:

"Died, at his residence in Winchester on Thursday, October 26th, 1876, Nicholas J. Towne, age 86 years. The deceased was born in New Jersey in 1790. His parents moved to Philadelphia and died when he was only eight years old. Thrown upon the world to make his way unaided, he went to sea as a sailor at the age of 12 years. After serving five years on the sea, he came on shore and learned a trade and worked at it the most of his life. In the War of 1812 he was captured on the ocean by the British and when set free upon American soil he was stripped of all, even his shoes being taken. He moved to the State of Ohio in 1817, where he remained until 1864, when he came to Winchester where he has ever since resided.

> He was for many years a member of the M.E. Church and died in that faith. His oldest surviving daughter (Susan) watched over him and waited on him during his sickness with untiring care, and did all in her power to make him comfortable. Funeral services were held by Rev. T.W. Thornburg, after which the remains were interred in the cemetery at this place."

Turner, James Ferris   b 7 Apr 1852   d 6 Mar 1853   11 m

James was the son of John R. and Julia Ann Turner.

Turner, John R.   b 1819   d 13 May 1859   40 y 5 d

According to information of a family tree on ancestry.com, John married Julia Ann Branch on May 8, 1845. On the 1850 census of Winchester, John R. is 32 and a merchant, Juliann is 24, Mary E. is 5 and F. Leroy is 2. Another daughter, Lucinda Irene was born in 1854.

Voris, Caroline   b 1850   d 21 Dec 1870   20 y

Winchester Journal, Dec. 23, 1870:

> "DIED__In this city, at the residence of her mother, of catarrh in the head on Wednesday evening, Dec. 21, 1870, MISS CAROLINE VORIS, aged about 20. The deceased had been severely sick for several months prior to her death. She bore her sufferings with the heroic fortitude of a martyr, and gave evidence of her hope of a blessed immortality."

Voris, Henry C.   b 1846   d 1868   22 y

Henry was a soldier of Co. G., 8th Indiana, during the Civil War.

He wrote a will on March 28, 1868 leaving everything to his "beloved wife" (unnamed) and a request that she educate their "dear babe" so far as her limited means would enable her to do." He was only 22 and must have been ill and expecting death to write a will so young.

Voris, James R.   b 1852   d 11 Mar, 1875   23 y

Obituary, Winchester Journal, March 17, 1875:

"James R. Vorhis, formerly a printer in this office, died of Consumption at Farmland last Thursday. His remains were brought here and interred on Friday last. Jim was a genial, good hearted boy, like many others his own worst enemy."

Voris, Michael P. 2ⁿᵈ Lt.   b 1840 ?   d ? after Mar 1872   ?

Michael served with his brother, Henry C., as a soldier, Co. G. 8ᵗʰ Indiana, during the Civil War.

Article, Winchester Journal, March 6, 1872:

"AMPUTATED__We regret to state that Mike Voris, who has been suffering for several months past with a sore foot, was compelled to undergo an amputation. The operation was performed by Drs. Bosworth and Jaqua on Wednesday of last week. The amputation was performed about three inches above the ankle joint, and the patient is getting along finely. The history of the case, as well as we have been able to gather it is as follows: While playing baseball last spring, Mike got his ankle severely sprained, and subsequently, in trying to get out of the way of a passing train, he got two bones in his ankle joint broken. He has used every effort to cure it, even visiting the Surgical Institute at Indianapolis and undergoing treatment there, but all to no purpose. The foot kept getting worse and worse, until he was compelled to part with it.

Mike served during the late war as a soldier, passing through several terrible battles unscathed. He is an industrious young man, depending upon his labor for support and the loss falls severely upon him. He is receiving close attention and will, we hope, soon be about again."

I was not able to find out Michael's death date or the cause of his death.

The four Voris siblings listed above were the children of Curtis and Sarah Lighty Voris, sometimes spelled Vorhis.

Curtis and Sarah were married in Randolph County January 2, 1835. Curtis had previously been married to Margaret Rhoads in 1827 in Randolph County, but the four deceased above are the children of Curtis and Sarah. On the 1830 census Curtis and Margaret had a son and a daughter.

On the 1850 census of Winchester, Curtis is 50 and a butcher, Sarah is 35, Eunice is 13, Michael is 10, Margaret is 9, Henry C. is 4 and Hannah C. is 1.

On the 1860 census Sarah is 45 and the head of household, Caroline is 10, James R. is 7, Jacob is 5 and Belldorah is 3.

On the 1870 census Sarah is 55, Michael is 30 and a huckster, Hannah is 20, James R. is 18, Jacob B. is 15 and Bell is 12.

The burial site for Curtis is unknown, but probably at the Old Winchester. He died sometime between the 1850 and 1860 census records.

CHAPTER SEVENTEEN

I AM PAUL WAY, PLEASE MEET MY FAMILY

My name is Paul Way. My brothers, Henry and William, my nephew, Robert and our good friend, William Diggs, came here from South Carolina in 1816. I then returned to Carolina in 1817 and brought back my family, my parents and several other families.

I remember almost everything about that first trip. It was in the spring and Indiana was not even a state yet. We were four men and a boy, leaving our home in Beauty Spot, South Carolina, starting off toward the Ohio River and the scarcely explored forests beyond it, to establish a new home in Indiana.

We weren't the only ones on the trails. Emigration was a sight to behold! Some came on horseback, some on foot. Some had a pack horse to carry their belongings. It was the hardiest and sturdiest of us who made it all the way to the forests of Randolph County.

We came cross country with a road wagon and crossed the Ohio River at Louisville, Kentucky. We had to cross when it was frozen over. When we got to our destination we built our first camp just west of what is now Winchester. There were mostly Indians living here. When William Diggs married Charlotte Way in October of 1816 the closest white settler lived 12 miles from them. The Indians were plentiful and peaceful. Fannie Diggs was the first white child born in White River, on September 11, 1817.

When the second group came back with me in May of 1817 the Ohio River was still frozen over. There were 27 of us total. We had followed Indian trails most of the way from Carolina, but when we got back close to Winchester there was 10 inches of snow. We traveled the last 15 miles with no trail to guide us. We entered several tracts of land and began clearing forest and building our cabins.

The cabins were built from round logs and clapboards. A small cabin had one door and one window and a large one might have two of each. The chimney and fireplace were outside. If there were any neighbors within a few miles they came and helped with the raising of a cabin. We were the first to come so we helped each other.

The way you got land was as follows: First, the land was ceded by the Indians. Then it was surveyed and patented by the United States. Then you had to pick your land, enter it and pay for it. When we arrived, the closest place to enter land was Cincinnati. Much of the earliest land was held by squatters. They could stay on the land if they wanted but they had to pay for it. Squatters often moved on westward and most settlers came to stay. Everyone was considered to be equal, everyone helped each other and were hospitable with each other. Most of us were Quakers who wanted to move north and west because we did not believe in slavery. We only brought with us the bare necessities like kettles and other ironware. Beds, featherbeds and furniture were usually not brought because they could be made. We did try to bring a year's worth of clothing, then clothing too was made from deerskin and later wool and linen (called linsey-woolsy).

After the cabin was up we started clearing the land. First planted was a corn field. All of our bread was made of corn at first. Then we planted a vegetable patch and then a flax patch that could be made into linen. We raised sheep early on to get the wool for clothing. Meat was in abundance in every direction....turkey, deer and wild hogs left by some Indians. We traded with Indians for moccasins. The axe to a settler was the tool for all work.

It didn't take long for us to organize into a community, even though we might be miles apart. The first tax in Randolph County was in May, 1819 and was 25 cents per horse. Money was needed only to buy iron, salt, and powder and lead for our guns. All other necessities were grown, made or traded.

We worked hard but there was time to play. The children played with Indian children and the men participated in sports with the Indians, like running races, heaving stones and like activities. We had hoe-downs with singing, laughing and joking. The women had spinning bees. Hunting was both work and sport.

Indiana became a state in 1816. In January of 1818 Randolph became a county and in August of the same year Winchester became the county seat. The growth of Winchester was slow but the population of the county grew rapidly from 1820-1830. During the almost 40 years I lived in Winchester I saw it grow from about four cabins in 1818 to a regular town by the time I died in 1856.

The town was bustling with business and successful in its prosperity. Houses were built, businesses were established, churches were built, and a government was developed. Travel was made easier with the development of roads and the town square became the center of government, shopping and entertainment.

My wife, Achsah (pronounced Ax-sa) Moorman and I raised our children, Anna, William, Caroline and Anderson here. I had many roles in Winchester's development. Probably I was best known for platting the city of Winchester. If you live within a few blocks of the town square in any direction my name will "In Memoriam. To the W.M., Wardens and Brethren of Winchester Lodge, No 56. F. and A.M. Your committee, appointed to prepare and submit a memorial of our deceased Brother, Squire Welker, *be on your abstract. I also laid out the state and county roads. I had a hotel, worked as a surveyor and farmer. I was a juror and a justice of the peace. And before I became an abolishionist many a good time was had at the Paul Way tavern.*

I lived to age 70 and Achsah to age 72, very old age for the time. We are now buried side by side at the Heaston Graveyard. We are grateful for our opportunity to be among the first white people here and to see our town grow and prosper.

I found the Ways a particularly enjoyable family to study. Of course, to study the Ways was also to study the Diggs and Moormans. Some were married to each other when they came, like Paul Way and Achsah Moorman and William Diggs and Charlotte Way. Since they were among the first white families of Winchester, they naturally married each other. I found a newspaper article on the internet that was published in the Farmland Enterprise, dated June 17, 1904. "The tenth annual reunion of the families of the Moormans, Diggs and Ways, was held last week at the grove of Henry A. Moorman, four miles east of Farmland, one of the best they have ever had." The article explained that the Diggs branch of the family were the descendants of Sir Dudley Diggs of England who settled in Virginia. Descendents of his came to Randolph County around 1820. The ancestors of the Moorman family came to America with William Penn and the Quakers, settling in Pennsylvania. The immediate ancestors of this family came to this county in 1818. The Way family are the descendants of Henry Way, the Puritan, who came to America in 1630. Family members settled first in Massachusetts, then to the island of Nantucket, then to South Carolina and from there to here in 1817. The article said that the intermarriage between the families explained the triune character of their reunions.

There is a lot of information about these three families available for research at the Randolph County Historical Society Museum, and considerable information on the internet and specifically at ancestry. com. Studying these families was a challenge because children were often named after parents, grandparents, aunts and uncles, resulting in name confusion generation to generation. I think I have them with their correct birth families, but wouldn't bet the bank on it!

Interestingly, no one by the last name of Diggs or Moorman is buried at the Old Winchester as far as my research has found. Some were buried there, but their remains were moved to Fountain Park when it was opened.

The following Ways are buried at the Old Winchester and are listed in alphabetical order:

Way, Achsah Moorman b 2 Sep 1786 d 1 Mar 1859 72 y 6 m 29 d

Way, Infant　　　　　b 1862　　　　d 10 Aug 1862　　　　? m

This was a son of A.D. and Susanah A. Way

Way, John　　　　　b 9 Dec 1778　　d 25 Sep 1856　　77 y 9 m 26 d

John was a brother of Paul and a son of William and Abigail Way. He was a soldier of the War of 1812 and a new military marker was placed in his honor.

Way, Mary Ann E. b 21 Jun 1848　　d 30 Aug 1876　28 y 2 m 5 d

On the 1850 census of White River Township, Randolph County, Jesse Way was 42 and clerking, Lucinda was 38, Henry was 14, Evaline was 11, Caroline was 9, William R. was 7, Thomas was 5 and Mary A.E. was 3.

On the 1860 census Jesse Way was 52 and a merchant, Lucinda was 50, Henry L. was 22, William R. was 17, Thomas J. was 14, Mary A.E. was 12, Huldah E. was 8 and James L. was 5.

Obituary, Winchester Journal, August 30, 1876:

"DIED__On Saturday morning last after a very short illness of Cerebro Spinal Meningitis, (spinal fever), Miss Mary Ann E. Way, daughter of Jesse Way. The deceased was born in this city June 21st, 1848, and was 28 years, 2 months and five days old at the time of her death. She was an affectionate daughter and leaves many friends to mourn her death. The procession that followed her remains to the tombs last Sabbath was one of the largest we have ever seen in Winchester."

Way, Patience Green   b 29 Dec 1789   d 22 Aug 1858   77 y

Winchester newspaper, August 22, 1858:

"DIED__August 22nd, after a protracted illness, PATIENCE WAY, widow of John Way, aged nearly 78 years."

Way, Paul   b 1786   d 20 Oct 1856   70 y 7 m 26 d

Paul and Achsah were on the 1830 census with five others, on the 1840 census they were without children living with them. Then on the 1850 census, Paul was 64 and a farmer, Achsah was 61, Anderson D. was 32, Susanah was 29 and Olive Viola was five months.

Way, Susanah   b 20 Apr 1820   d 19 Aug 1862   42 y 3 m 29 d

On their marriage record in Randolph County, Anderson D. Way married Susanah Eltzroth February 12, 1849.

Way, William   b ?   d 9 Apr 1839   83 y

Way, Abigail   b ?   d 2 Jan 1829   73 y

William and Abigail are the oldest of the Ways to migrate from South Carolina. They are the parents of Paul, John, Henry and William (and probably others). Buried on the family farm, years later their children placed a monument in their memory in the Old Winchester. It was not found during the restoration process, but I list them here as their children would have wished.

CHAPTER EIGHTEEN

WEAVER, MRS. JACOB – WRIGHT, INFANT

Weaver, Mrs. Jacob   b ?   d 2 May 1880   ? y

Winchester Journal, May 5, 1880:

> "Mrs. Weaver, widow of Jacob Weaver, an aged lady living in the west part of the town died last Sunday. Her funeral occurred yesterday."

I could not find them on any census records. Her husband may also be buried at the Old Winchester.

Welker, Martha Brown "Mattie"   b 1839   d 6 Aug 1890   51 y

Winchester Journal article, May 26, 1886:

> "Mrs. Welker, widow of Squire Welker, has been placed on the pension roles at the rate of $12 per month…….."

Obituary, Winchester Journal, August 14, 1890:

"Mrs. Mattie Welker, whose illness has been mentioned in these columns, died last Thursday. Her remains were interred at the old cemetery beside those of her husband, on Friday, after services conducted by Elder I.P Watts at the Main Street Christian Church."

In Martha's last will and testament, dated July 23, 1888, she left everything to her sister, Sarah E. Parker.

Welker, Squire   b 30 May 1829   d 15 Jul 1885   56 y 1 m 15 d

Squire was a soldier in Co. H., 84th Indiana. He enlisted August 7, 1862 and mustered out June30, 1865. We placed a new military marker as a memorial during the restoration.

On the 1870 census of Winchester Squire is 36 and a cabinet maker and Martha is 32. They did not list any children.

Death Notice, Winchester Journal, July 22, 1885:

"The funeral of the late Squire Welker took place last Friday afternoon. He was buried at the old cemetery with the honors of Masonry, and his remains were followed by a large procession of friends. He was a good soldier as well as a citizen, and was highly respected. Obituary notice next week."

Obituary, Winchester Journal:

"In Memoriam. To the W.M., Wardens and Brethren of Winchester Lodge, no.56. F. and A. M. Your committee, appointed to prepare and submit a memorial to our deceased Brother, Squire Welker, submit the following report: Squire Welker was born in Knox County, Ohio, May 30, 1829. He remained in the county of his nativity until the fall of 1848 when he moved to Perry County, same state. He remained there until April 1, 1850 when he moved to Winchester, where he resided until his death.

On the 7th day of August, 1862, he enlisted in Capt. Geo. U. Carter's Company H of the 84th Regiment, Indiana Volunteers. He served with this command undergoing all of the dangers and privations incident to a soldier's life until he was attacked with disease at War Trace, Tenn., from which he never recovered sufficiently to rejoin his regiment; but was transferred to company 155 of the Veteran Reserve Corps on the 22nd day of April, 1864, and served in that corps until June 30, 1865, when he was discharged at the close of the war.

He was married to Miss Martha Brown, who survives him, March 10th, 1867. Two children were the fruits of this Union, both of whom preceded Brother Welker to the Spirit Land.

Bro. Welker was made a Mason in Wapello Lodge No. 5, Iowa, at some time in the year 1854, your committee being unable to ascertain the exact date. He joined this Lodge on dimit from Wapello Lodge, January 22, 1861, and remained an honored member until his death.

Brother Welker never recovered his health lost in the service of his country and his wife has been an invalid confined to her room for many years. These afflictions bore heavily upon our deceased Brother, but he bore them cheerfully and uncomplainingly, and ever had a pleasant greeting for all with whom he came in contact. His health was such that he could not endure hard labor, but he was an industrious man, doing whatever his hands found to do to maintain those dependent upon him.

While Bro. Welker's afflictions were such that he could not often attend the meetings of the Lodge and enjoy the society of his brethren, he was devoted to the principles of our beloved order and lived up to its teachings. In his death the lodge has lost a true and honored member; his wife a loving tender and devoted husband, the community an honest and upright citizen, and the country a true patriot and brave defender.

Bro. Welker died Wednesday, July 15, 1885, aged 56 years, 1 month and 15 days. His remains were deposited in the family burial lot adjoining the old cemetery at his place, on Friday, July 17th, 1885, with the honors of Masonry, after appropriate services by our Brother Elder I.P. Watts, there to await the final resurrection, when land and sea shall give up their dead. Your Committee recommends that the Secretary set apart a memorial page on the records of this lodge in honor of our deceased brother and that he furnish a copy of this report to each of the papers published in Winchester, with the request that they publish the same, and also furnish a copy to the widow of our deceased brother. Fraternally Submitted A.C. Beeson, A.J. Winter, R. Bosworth."

Wells, Unknown Children of B.F. and A. A.

Wells, Charles Quincy   b 1871   d 3 Aug 1872   10 m 10 d

Winchester Journal, August 14, 1872:

"Near Winchester, on Saturday evening, August 3rd, 1872, of teething diarrhea, Charles Quincy, son of B.F. and A.A Wells, aged 10 months and ten days. Our little bud of promise has been transplanted to bloom in paradise."

The sadness for Benjamin and Amelia Wells had to have been very great, as they lost five children to death at young ages. We restored a stone for four of the children, none of whom were named on the gravestone. We did not find a gravestone for Charles, but believe with certainty that he is also buried at the Old Winchester.

On the 1900 census of White River Township, Randolph County, Benjamin F. is 65, Amelia A. is 59 and one daughter, Etta Wells, age 29, is living with them. I do not know if they had other children who survived to adulthood.

Wesp, Philibum   b 1869   d 23 Apr 1872   3 y

Winchester Journal, April 24, 1872:

"John Wesp's little three year old daughter died yesterday from the effects of the measles."

On the 1870 census of Winchester, John Wesp is listed as working in the mills, and being born in Germany, Mary is 30, Henry is 7, Rosana C. is 5 and Philibum is 9 months.

Wilson, Miss Rebecca   b 1817   d 28 Jan 1880   63 y

Obituary, Winchester Journal, February 4, 1880:

"DIED__In this city, on Wednesday last, MISS REBECCA WILSON, aged nearly 63 years. The deceased had be afflicted with dropsy for nearly two years, and suffered much, but bore up with Christian fortitude. The funeral services were conducted by Rev. Elkanah Beard last Thursday, after which the remains were interred in the old cemetery. The deceased was born near

> Johnson's Station, this county, removed to Winchester when a small girl, and remained here until her death."

I was unable to find any additional information about Rebecca.

Woody, John Eberle   b 1840   d 3 Mar 1859   19 y 4 m4 d

John was the son of Dr. Robert and Caroline Way Woody. I did not learn a cause of death.

Woody, Caroline   b 1816   d ?   34-44 y

Caroline was the wife of Dr. Robert Woody.

On the 1850 census of White River Township, Randolph County, Robert is 41 and a physician, Caroline is 34, William is 14, Eberle is 10 and (can't read) male is 6.

On the 1860 census of Washington Township, Preble County, Ohio, Robert Woody is 52, M.D., married to Abigail Woody age 47. No children are listed.

On the 1870 census of Preble County, Ohio, Robert is 62, Abigail is 58 and they have resident boarders.

So Caroline had to have died sometime between the 1850 and 1860 census reports.

An announcement of the death of Dr. Woody was in the Winchester paper on September 27, 1871.

> "At his residence, near Eaton, Ohio on Saturday, last, Dr. Robert Woody, aged 63 years. The Dr. was for many years a practicing physician in this place. He was one of the earliest settlers of this

County, and left but a few years since to remove to the home in which he died. His death was caused by a complication of diseases, and he was sadly afflicted for some weeks before his death. The deceased was a brother-in-law of Nathan Reed, Esq."

(Nathan's wife, Anna, and Robert's wife, Caroline, were sisters, the daughters of Paul and Achsah Way.)

Wright, Infant   b 1846   d 30 Sep 1846   ? m

This infant was a son of Edward and Mary A. Heaston Wright.

They were married in Randolph County on December 21, 1837.

On the 1850 census Edward is 34 and a farmer, Mary Ann is 31, Catherine is 11, Eliza Ann is 8, Nancy is 6 and Mary Ann is 2.

CHAPTER NINETEEN

THE WYSONGS

The Wysongs were among the first white people to settle in the Winchester area, coming here in 1817 or 1818.

A descendent, Mrs. Fred Miller, gave a talk to the Randolph County Historical Society on January 22, 1967, and I found a copy of her talk at the museum. Some of the information in this chapter is from her talk. There is also historical information about the Wysongs in the History of Randolph County 1882 by E. Tucker and genealogy information on ancestry.com and other web sites.

Valentine Wysong and his wife, Elizabeth Albright, both of German descent, moved to the wilderness of Indiana from Pennsylvania by way of Virginia and Ohio. They did this traveling with their nine children who were Valentine Jr., Jacob, Joseph, Henry, Lewis, John, Elizabeth, Catherine and David. Valentine was a brick mason by trade and had considerable property and finances for those times.

This chapter is primarily about the youngest of their children, David. He was born in Virginia April 3, 1799. In Tucker's History David is listed many times. Among "first things", David is credited with firing the first brick in these parts, the bricks used for the second courthouse built in 1826. In the records of the Commissioner's Court it states "David Wysong has contracted for building a new court house;

the price does not appear. He is allowed $225 extra for a rock foundation instead of brick."

In a section of Tucker's book called "Reminiscences", Solomon Wright said that Paul Way surveyed the town plat and David Wright "cried" (auctioned) the lots at the first sale. Mr. Wright stated, talking about David Wysong, "That young man is good-looking, and he would look better still if he would just bid a little higher."

David is also mentioned in Tucker's History among "early settlers", "prominent families" and as a businessman. In 1861 David attended the first meeting of the Old Settlers.

He married Eliza Irvin, the daughter of John and Margaret Irvin, who came here from Virginia. They lived on a farm about three-fourths mile from town on what was later called Hog-Back road (or Pike). Although David was primarily a farmer, he is best known in Winchester history for building the second court house. Started in 1826, it apparently was not completed by the May term of court in 1839. Finally Michael Aker was contracted to finish the job. (The first court house was a log cabin used from about 1820-1826 when it was sold by the Commissioners to David Heaston for a hotel. Paul Way bought it from Mr. Heaston and ran it as a hotel for many years.) David Wysong was on the stand at the dedication of the third (and present) courthouse dedication is 1877. The third courthouse was originally built for $73,000 plus $4,900 for a heating system.

David and Eliza lived isolated in the wilderness, building their home and barn. The men at that time hewed and hacked away at the wilderness with their axes and the women cooked and sewed and spun and wove....and had babies, lots of them usually. David and Eliza were the parents of twelve children (or more, it's unclear). Their children were named Harvey, Elizabeth, Margaret, Irvin, Perry, Henry, Jefferson, Caroline, Mariah, Ellen, Joseph and Franklin.

Eliza died in 1853 and is buried in the Old Winchester. Her tombstone has been found and restored. David later married Rebecca Morrison Hill and when she died he took for his third wife Mary Edwards Pugh. David resided in the family homestead for nearly 60 years where he died April 12, 1878. He is buried with Eliza at the Old Winchester. I do not know where his second and third wives are buried but they are not on the list for the Old Winchester.

Harvey Wysong the oldest child of David and Eliza, followed in his father's footsteps learning the brick mason trade. Harvey laid the brick for our present courthouse as well as the jail built in 1881, the Asahel Stone mansion, the Moorman home on South Main (which burned) and other buildings on the public square.

Every family has at least one mystery to try to solve. There is one source found in historical papers that indicate that four Wysong children of David and Eliza are buried in the Old Winchester. On the 1850 census May Jane (age 9) and Sarah (age 4) are listed among the children and apparently they did not reach adulthood, but they were still alive on the 1860 census. Another child, Thomas Jefferson Wysong, apparently did not reach adulthood either. I could not find a fourth name. I will leave it to future researchers or descendents to fill in the blanks.

The Wysongs put their stamp on Randolph County and the City of Winchester. I wonder what David and his son, Harvey, would think about the recent restoration and expansion of their courthouse and its cost?

Wysong, David   b 3 Apr 1799   d 26 Apr 1878   79 y 23 d

On the 1850 census of White River Township, Randolph County, David is 49 and a farmer. Eliza is 41, Irvin, 22, Mariah, 18, Perry, 16, Henry, 14, Caroline, 11, Mary Jane ,9, Thomas J., 6, Sarah E., 4 and Joseph B., 6 months.

Franklin was born in 1851 and is thought to be the last child of David and Eliza. As an adult he and his family lived in the Wysong estate home, willed to him by his father.

On both the 1860 and 1870 census reports David is listed as a widower.

Winchester Journal, May 1, 1878:

"DIED___At his residence South of this city, on Friday last, after a long and painful illness, DAVID WYSONG, aged 79 years and 23 days. The deceased was born in Franklin County, Va., and came to this County in 1818; he resided near where he settled until his death. He was one of the oldest pioneers of the County, of whom but few are living. Funeral services were held at the M.E. Church by Rev. M. Crosley, of Fort Wayne, on Monday last, his text being from John 16, chap., 2nd verse, and Second Cor., 4th chap., 16th verse. The funeral was a very large one, very many being unable to gain admission to the house. The Emersonians and the new band kindly furnished music for the occasion."

David left a long and detailed will leaving most of his considerable assets to his son, Franklin, who was also named executor of his will. He left him all of the real estate that he owned as well as some land he had purchased in Kansas. He left specific amounts of money to his other children who were still living at the time of his death, namely Henry, Thomas J, Joseph, Caroline, Maria Hulingh, Margaret Wright, Ellen Hiatt, and Irvin and Perry if there was any money left.

Wysong, Eliza   b 1 Aug 1807   d 29 Dec 1853   46 y 4 m 28 d

Eliza and David were married in Randolph County on April 19, 1822.

She came to Randolph County with her family from Virginia around 1818, about the same time David moved here with his family. Her father was John Irvin, married to Margaret, also a native of Virginia. John Irvin was a carpenter and a house painter.

Chapter Twenty

Remains Moved to Fountain Park Cemetery
Alphabetical Listing

The remains of persons buried in Fountain Park Cemetery who died prior to or during early 1880 had to have been moved from some other burial site. To aid researchers those persons are listed here alphabetically. Further research may help determine exact death dates and burial sites, but this book is about those who remain buried in the Old Winchester Graveyard, not those whose remains were moved. The Randolph County Historical Society Museum has microfilm of old area newspapers that may contain obituaries for some of the people listed along with other information that may be of interest to genealogists.

Name	Death or Burial Date
Alexander, Eliza E.	04-25-1865
Alexander, Martin	??-??-1876
Allen, Catherine and Eddie**	02-17-1866
Allen, Evaline**	10-24-1870
Allen, Joseph B.**	02-24-1865

Badgley, Abigail**	01-27-1881
Badgley, Joseph**	02-09-1859
Badgley, Rebecca*	02-09-1859
Bailey, David D.*	02-17-1870
Baldwin, John W.	07-28-1871
Baldwin, Samuel A. *	03-09-1877
Bales, Mary E.	11-07-1861
Batchfield, Christian**	03-11-1877
Bates, Harry A.	10-09-1865
Browne, Ruth	03-10-1879
Browne, Sarah Jane**	03-24-1875
Brown, Thomas M.	04-23-1876
Bruce, Cindrilla	07-31-1866
Bruce, George Ann	06-03-1864
Bruce, Timandria	05-31-1866
Campbell, Sarah Ann	07-25-1865
Carter, Edmund D.**	??-??-1873
Carver, Arthur R.	10-06-1877
Carver, Henry	??-??-1872
Cheney. Lillie M**.	??-??-1862
Cheney, Mary**	??-??-1877

Clark, Barbara	03-25-1874
Clear, Cornelius	07-13-1871
Clear, John	04-06-1865
Clenney, Mary A.	??-??-1881
Clenney, William L	??-??-1870
Comer, Elizabeth**	??-??-1879
Cottom, Cora E.	11-16-1854
Cox, Theodore F**.	??-??-??
Cox, Zeruah	??-??-1858
Cronnenwelt, Andrew**	02-16-1881
Curry, Charles M.	??-??-1874
Daly, Charles B.C.	??-??-1850
Daly, George W.	??-??-1868
Darrah, Martha	??-??-1875
Darrah, Thomas	??-??-1849
Deardorf, Lafayette**	09-??-1875
Deardorf, Mrs. Lafayette	??-??-??
Deem, India Goodrich	01-25-1869
Diggs, Agnes	02-02-1839
Diggs, Bessie	??-??-1878
Diggs, Charlotte	01-31-1877

Diggs, Littleberry C.	12-21-1849
Diltz, Charlie W.	12-16-1862
Dubree, Mary Owens	??-??-??
Edwards, Eli	07-29-1880
Edwards, Elizabeth*	12-26-1863
Edwards, Elizabeth**	??-??-1871
Edwards, Jonathan**	07-16-1870
Eltzroth, Mary	11-22-1856
Emsley, Elmer	09-05-1869
Ennis, Elizabeth Wilcox	??-??-1857
Ennis, John	??-??-1879
Evans, Mary Elizabeth*	05-24-1875
Evans, Tommy W.*	10-29-1876
Fleming, J.W.	??-??-1862
Fletcher, Ellen	02-??-1879
Fletcher, George**	??-??-??
Fox, George	07-26-1866
Fudge, Josie	03-30-1879
Gallaher, Caroline	12-15-1876
Goodrich, Edmund B.	02-04-1843

Goodrich, Ellen N. 09-10-1833

Goodrich, John B.** 11-29-1872

Hancock, Henry 09-05-1876

Hay, Catherine** 03-26-1876

Hay, George** 05-15-1878

Heaston, Abraham** 04-15-1870

Heaston, Christian** 09-06-1877

Heaston, Emma 09-28-1872

Heaston, George W. 07-02-1867

Heaston, Nathaniel 08-28-1874

Heaston, S.P.** 03-05-1864

Heaston, Sarah** 05-01-1866

Heltz, Mae 06-23-1880

Hiatt, Effa M. 08-26-1869

Hobbick, Christian** 04-08-1868

Hobbick, Christina** 06-22-1862

Hodson, Beatrice 02-25-1873

Hoffman, Dollie** 05-23-1874

Hoffman, Kattie** 06-02-1872

Honour, Mathias 11-22-1846

Houser, James** 04-30-1879

Hull, Jehiel* 11-10-1874

Hull, Polly**	06-17-1867
Hull, Stephen J.**.	??-??-??
Hull, William E.**	??-??-??
Husten, John A.	02-07-1867
Jaqua, David G.	??-??-1844
Jaqua, Elbridge	??-??-1853
Jaqua, Jesse B.	??-??-1871
Jaqua, Mary J.	??-??-1872
Jaqua, Thomas	??-??-1850
Jarrett, Emily*	02-26-1872
Jenkinson, Isabel	??-??-1864
Jenkinson, John	??-??-1868
Kelley, Dennis	05-07-1871
Kelley, Frank A.**	03-27-1875
Kelley, Lydia S.	04-01-1874
Kelley, Mary L.	09-15-1870
Kelley, Mary S.	05-04-1866
Kemp, Sarah E.	01-??-1876
Kizer, Abe Lincoln	04-03-1863
Kizer, Adam	09-07-1826
Kizer, Cabel	08-26-1828

Kizer, Elias   03-05-1867

Kizer, Frances Ellen   08-22-1851

Kizer, Henry   08-12-1823?

Kizer, Margery   10-30-1869

Kizer, Sarah   08-13-1823

Kizer, Susannah   01-15-1874

(The above members of the Kizer family were moved from a burial ground on the family farm.)

Kizer, Daniel   10-07-1854

Kiser, Infant Daughter of W.D.   ??-??-1880

Kiser, Infant Son of W.D.   ??-??-1876

Kizer, Sarah Ann   07-10-1850

Kizer, William   11-20-1859

Lafferty, Winnie**   02-20-1875

Lafferty, Thomas**   01-??-1876

Lucas, Rev. S.H.**   10-31-1860

Ludy, Margaret   09-17-1862

Lykins, Jonas**   08-15-1876

Magee, William   01-14-1874

McAdams, Annie   ??-??-1864

McAdams, Frank Elmer**   ??-??-1877

McAdams, Rosalie	??-??-1879
McClure, Samuel M**.	04-14-1873
McDonald, Mary E.**	10-06-1874
Miller, Bessie J.	??-??-1877
Miller, Ella	02-12-1879
Miller, Eunice	02-24-1870
Miller, Ferma	??-??-1871
Miller, Infant son of W.T.	08-25-1872
Miller, Infant son of W.T.	02-26-1870
Monks, Emma C.	02-21-1861
Monks, John**	01-09-1865
Monks, Mary A.**	03-25-1866
Monks,William	10-08-1876
Moon, Jacob	03-25-1872
Moore, James	07-12-1875
Moorman, Agnes	10-13-1860
Moorman, Jessie	08-26-1839
Moorman, Tarleton	09-22-1860
Moorman, W.D.	12-26-1848
Mullen, Ellis**	11-18-1874
Mullen, Etta**	11-25-1862
Mullen, Mary A.**	06-09-1862
Mullin, Susan	??-??-1863

Murray, Garland	??-??-1868
Murray, Isaac	08-??-1860
Murray, Margaret	06-??-1851
Needham, Emsley	??-??-1872
Needham, Estella	??-??-1863
Needham, Frederick	??-??-1865
Neff, Allen O.**	12-27-1880
Neff, Elizabeth	05-21-1862
Neff, Infant son of H.H.&M.M.**	11-22-1866
Neff. John S.	07-??-1850
Neff ,J. Lawrence**	03-10-1865
Neff, Rosa ??-??-1877	
Nixon, Mary	05-29-1857
O'Harra, Lydia Ellen	09-03-1879
Owens, Elizabeth	??-??-??
Owens, Mathew	12-29-1858
Oyler, Sarah	01-18-1867
Phillips, Ford C.	01-08-1979
Preston, Samuel**	01-21-1874
Puckett, Benjamin	08-09-1973

Puckett, Hardy	02-23-1849
Puckett, Jehu	08-27-1868
Puckett, Levi	10-10-1872
Puckett, Sarah	07-23-1849
Puckett, Willie	02-23-1878
Ramsey, David J.	09-03-1876
Ramsey, Infant Elsie	03-??-1878
Ramsey, Janet	10-28-1858
Ramsey, Johney	12-??-1879
Ramsey, Mary J.	10-17-1863
Reed, Anna*	03-25-1872
Reed, Erastus H.*	08-20-1864
Reed, James E*.	05-17-1857
Reinheimer, Pearl	??-??-1880
Remmel, Levi	08-08-1876
Richardson, Cynthia S.& infant	05-12-1853
Richardson, Ellen F	07-06-1859
Richardson, Mary J.	??-??-??
Roosa, Husten R.	08-28-1880
Ross, Dr. A.L.**	01-29-1877
Rowes, Infant Fredrick	02-19-1877

Rowes, Fredrick	03-04-1879
Ruble, Samuel	11-28-1841
Seagraves, Frankie	??-??-1878
Seagraves, Zoe E.	08-??-1871
Scott, Hannah	??-??-1876
Shaw, Child**	??-??-??
Stakebake, Anna Clark	04-16-1866
Stakebake, George	04-10-1854
Stakebake, John	12-29-1853
Stanley, P.A.	12-11-1875
Steele, Agustus**	??-??-??
Steele, Anna**	??-??-1863
Steele, James A.**	??-??-1863
Steele, James W.	??-???-1870
Steele, Lt. William L.**	05-16-1863
Stephens, Mrs. Elijah	11-12-1880
Stone, Ezra**	08-23-1848
Summers, Annie	??-??-1850
Summers, Charles	12-06-1874
Summers, Susanna**	09-15-1847

Tharp, Nancy J.	09-24-1851
Thomas, Martin R.**	08-10-1863
Tooker, Mary E. & baby	02-26-1871
Wallace, Infant	10-??-1878
Ward, Eudora	11-13-1860
Ward, Jane Helen	06-07-1865
Ward, Jane Helen	08-11-1868
Ward, Sarah Ellen	09-03-1852
Ward, Susan Lykins	02-08-1873
Ward, Susan	08-24-1873
Way, Amy Elta**	07-01-1864
Way, Ellen**	03-09-1867
Way, Fred L.	08-12-1873
Way, Hannah M. Martin**	??-??-??
Way, Henry T.	04-02-1868
Way, Mary**	??-??-1858
Way, Mathew**	08-29-1849
Way, Robert	10-18-1874
Way, Startling	12-29-1855
Way, Wilson T.	10-29-1855
Williamson, Catharine	05-29-1869
Wilmore, Helen M.	05-06-1874

Wilmore, James W.**	05-06-1867
Wilmore, Sarah F.**	02-12-1863
Wilmore, William H.	??-??-1871
Winchell, Maud J.	01-30-1876
Winter, Mary H.	02-24-1878
Wright, A.W.	??-??-1880
Wright, Edward	08-23-1880
Wright, Eva	??-??-1878
Wysong, Lillie	??-??-1878
Wysong, Mary M.	06-02-1875

Memorial markers have been found in both Old Winchester and Fountain Park Cemeteries. It is uncertain where the remains are actually buried.

** *Known to have been moved from the old Winchester to the Fountain Park Cemetery by documentation available at the Randolph County Historical Museum*

CHAPTER TWENTY-ONE

OBITUARY AND GRAVEYARD CLUES

Old obituaries are interesting and informational to read, but they can also be confusing. I spent many a day going through the microfilm of old Winchester newspapers looking for death notices and obituaries, and found many more than expected. Occasionally I would find a word or abbreviation that left me wondering, "Now what in the world does that mean?" I searched out some answers that were helpful, so I hope they will be to you also.

First, there is the word "relic". In the language of the period of the Old Winchester Graveyard, a relic was the survivor (usually a widow) of a marriage union.

A "consort" is a partner, and in the case of a death, a female who leaves a surviving spouse. An easy way to remember the term consort is to think of a marriage as a consortium between a husband and wife.

"Spinster" and " bachelor" simply referred to unmarried females and males.

"Inst." is used frequently in the obituaries and is a term that refers to a recent occurrence in the present or current month. It is an abbreviation for instant.

I don't recall running into this situation in my research, but it is useful to know that prior to 1752, when the American colonies adopted the Gregorian calendar, the first month of the year was not January. The year started with the Spring Equinox in the middle of March.

Also included here are inscriptions and artwork found on tombstones, and an explanation of what those usually mean. This will be helpful when you take a walk through the graveyard, and I hope you do.

I found this information online at freepages.genealogy.rootsweb. ancestry.com/~familyhistorypages/InscriptionsExplain.

Religious :

Angels – Angels mean spirituality and they guard the tomb.

Bible - A single Holy Bible is often found on Christian stones.

Chalice – Usually used to represent the Sacraments.

Crown – The soul's achievement and the Glory of life after death.

Cross – The Cross is an emblem of faith. There are many different types of crosses and each may mean something different.

Heart – Often found in Catholic cemeteries, the sacred heart refers to the suffering of Christ for our sins.

Mortality:

Arrow – Mortality.

Broken Column – This image represents the decay. It usually represents the loss of the head of the family.

Candle being snuffed – Loss of life.

Hourglass – Time has run out.

Spade or Crossed Spade and Shovel – Death.

Trade and Occupation:

Barber – Bowl and razor.

Butcher – An axe, steel knife or cleaver.

Farmer – A coulter (type of hoe), flail (threshing implement), swing-tree (rod for beating flax) or stock of corn.

Brick Mason – Wedge and level.

Merchant – Scales, some type of sign.

Minister – Bible.

Blacksmith – Crown, hammer and anvil.

Teacher – An open book.

Weaver – A loom, or shuttle and stretchers.

Resurrection, Eternal Life, Immortality:

Angel, flying or trumpeting – Rebirth, resurrection.

Bird or Bird Flying – Eternal life, resurrection.

Dove, Flying – Resurrection.

Flame, Light, Lamp or Torch – Immortality of the Spirit, resurrection.

Garland or Wreath – Symbol of saintliness and glory, victory in death.

Ivy – Immortality

Star – Death could not overpower the Light of the Spirit which still shines in the darkness.

Urn - Immortality

Animals:

Birds – Eternal life or resurrection.

Butterfly – Short life

Dog – Implies a good master worthy of love.

Dove – Seen in both Christian and Jewish cemeteries, the dove means innocence or peace.

Lamb – Usually marks the grave of a child and means innocence. (There are many lambs in the Old Winchester Graveyard.)

Plants:

Fruits – Eternal plenty as in the fruit of life.

Full-bloom rose – The deceased died in the prime of life.

Ivy – Ivy stands for friendship as well as immortality.

Laurel – A symbol of worldly accomplishment and heroism.

Lily – A symbol of purity and innocence.

Morning Glory – Signifies the beginning of life.

Oak, Oak Leaves and Acorns – Oak leaves can stand for power, au-thority or victory and are often seen on military tombs.

Palm branch – Signifies victory and rejoicing.

Poppy – Eternal sleep.

Roses – Signify completion and the brevity of earthly existence.

Rosemany – Rosemary is for remembrance. Thistles can also stand for remembrance. A thistle can also mean that the deceased is of Scottish descent.

Tree or Trees:

Tree – Stands for life.

Sprouting Tree – Stands for life everlasting.

Tree trunk – Stands for the brevity of life.

Weeping Willow – Perpetual mourning, grief. (There are several stones with weeping willows in the Old Winchester Graveyard.)

Wheat strands or sheaves – The divine harvest.

Hands:

Hand pointing up- Pathway to heaven.

Hands clasped – Farewells or the bond of marriage.

Hands praying – Asking God for eternal life.

Hands blessing – Blessing of those left behind.

Miscellaneous:

Harp – Praise to the God.

Heart- Love, stylized hearts stand for the affection of the living for the dead. Two joined hearts on a stone mark a marriage.

Rod or Staff – Comfort for the bereaved.

Stars and Stripes around an eagle – Eternal vigilance and liberty, often seen on military markers.

Urn with flame – Undying remembrance.

Broken ring – The family circle has been severed.

Cherub – Cherubs are angelic and signify innocence.

Crossed swords – Military person of high rank.

G.A. R. – Grand Army of the Republic

There are many symbols other than those listed. Fraternal organizations like the Masons, Elks, I.O.O.F and others have their specific symbols that are easy to find on the computer, but hard to describe without a picture.

I am including in this chapter some cautions for people who visit cemeteries and have trouble reading the carvings and epitaphs. Please use only water to clean any stone. Any other cleaning solution may be harmful to the stone. Also, please do not use chalk or shaving cream to make reading the stones easier since both are also harmful. I got some great advice from a website called the Connecticut Gravestone Network. They recommend that you learn to use a mirror to light a stone that is in the shade or is difficult to read. It is amazing how helpful this is in reading grave stones.

Chapter Twenty – Two

Articles and Items from
Early Winchester Newspapers

As I was going through the microfilm of old Winchester newspapers, my eyes were often drawn to certain advertisements and stories. I am including some of them here because they are reflective of the times when the people listed in this book were alive. Some are informative and some are humorous. Because of the poor quality of the print directly from the microfilm, I have elected to retype them here so that you do not get eye strain. All are typed as written. You are encouraged to go to the Randolph County Historical Museum and find the ad or article in the paper on the date listed and peruse the microfilm. If you do, I bet you will be there several hours later still reading!

2-28-1872

A drunken gipsey woman was the sensation at the prayer meeting of the M.E. church on Wednesday evening last. She pulled out a bottle of whisky and took a drink before proceeding with her devotions, for which she was summarily ejected from the Church. She then went to Gil Shaw's where she behaved herself so badly that she was put out of the house and taken before Squire Reed. She was put in jail over night, and released in the morning, under the promise that she would leave town at once and not return again. Upon being released she stood not upon the order of going, but "lit out" at once.

5-26- 1875

Program for Decoration Day

The citizens of Winchester and all others who desire to participate or be presented at the decoration of the graves of the soldiers of the late rebellion are respectfully requested to meet at the cemetery next Sabbath, May 30, at 10 o'clock A.M. The Sabbath Schools that meet in the morning are invited and requested, under the direction of their officers, immediately after the close of their morning exercises, to march in procession to the cemetery. The exercises of the day are:

1. Opening

2. Music by the choir

3. Prayer by Rev. J.G. Brice

4. Music by the choir

5. Decoration of the graves of the fallen heroes

6. Address by Revs. W.O. Pierce and Henry A. Merrill

7. Music by the German choir

8. Address by Elder Morrison

9. Address by Rev. J. Brewer in German

10. Music by the choir

11. Benediction

Should the weather be unfavorable for outdoor exercises, arrangements have been made for holding the meeting at City Hall, where the order of exercises will be gone through as given above except for the decorations. By order of THE COMMITTEE OF ARRANGEMENTS.

2-11-1858

Rules for Home Education

1. From your children's earliest infancy, inculcate the necessity of instant obedience.

2. Unite firmness with gentleness. Let your children always understand that you mean what you say.

3. Never promise them anything unless you are quite sure you can give them what you say.

4. If you tell a child to do something, show them how to do it; and see that it is done.

5. Always punish your children for willfully disobeying you, but never punish them in anger.

6. Never let them perceive that they can vex you or make you lose your self-composure.

7. If they give way to petulance and ill temper, wait till they are calm and then gently reason with them on the impropriety of their conduct.

8. Remember that a little present punishment, when occasion arises, is much more effectual than the threatening of a greater punishment should the fault be renewed.

9. Never give your children anything because they cry for it.

10. On no account allow them to do at one time what you have forbidden, under the same circumstances at another.

11. Teach them that the only sure and easy way to appear good is to be good.

12. Accustom them to make their little recitals with perfect truth.

13. Never allow tale-bearing.

14. Teach them self-denial, not self-indulgence of an angry and resentful spirit.

If these rules were reduced to practice - by parents and guardians, how much misery would be prevented - and how many in danger of ruin would be saved-how largely would the happiness of a thousand domestic circles be augmented! It is lamentable to see how extensive is parental neglect, and to witness the bad and dreadful consequences in the ruin of thousands. (Valley Farmer)

3-27-1863

The amount of money to be paid into the U.S. Treasury for exemption from military duty by the Quakers of Indiana, it is said, will amount to about $253,000.

Advertisement: Randolph County Seminary, John Cooper, Principal

The next term of this institution will commence of Monday, 13th of April, 1863 and continue for eleven weeks. TUITION PER TERM: Primary Department.....$4.00; Academic Department, Junior Class......$6.00; Middle Class......$8.00; Senior Class......$10.00. No deductions for absence, except in case of sickness. Tuition is due at the middle of the term. THOMAS W. KIZER, G.S. GOODRICH, A.H.HARRIS, EDWARD EDGER, JAMES BROWN, Trustees. Winchester, March 27, 1863

1-6-1865

JAMES ROUTH: We called last Monday, to see James Routh, of the 5th Indiana Cavalry, who were captured on the 11th day of July, and taken to Andersonville, Georgia, and turned into the slaughter pen. Mr. Routh comfirms all that has been said in reference to rebel barbarity. The scoundrels searched all the Yankee prisoners before they arrived at Andersonville, and took everything they had of value, but after they were turned into the slaughter pen, they were stripped of all their clothes to see if they had anything secreted about their persons, taking overcoats, boots, hats and blankets. They were furnished two ounces corn or raw beans, or in its stead, rice or mush. The meat furnished was rotten, that none but starved men could or would eat. They were taken from Andersonville on the 8th day of September, sent to Charleston and turned into the jail, under the fire of our own artillery from the forts, where they remained two days. They were then sent out west of the city, to the race track, where some of the women brought some vegetables to them but the Colonel in command refused to let them have these articles. They were sent to Florence on the 6th of October, where they remained until exchanged. He says at Andersonville there were seventy-five blood hounds to run down Union men who would escape; he saw some of our men torn pretty badly by dogs, who attempted to escape. A large number of our men took the oath of allegiance to the Rebel Government, rather than stay there and die from starvation. Mr. Routh weighed 165 lbs. when put into the rebel slaughter pen, and when he came out he weighed 85 lbs.

4-1873

L.G. PUCKETT DENTIST

TWENTY DOLLARS for an upper or lower set of teeth on rubber; best quality. One dollar and upward for gold fillings; twenty-five cents for extracting one tooth without gas. All dental work warranted. L.G. Puckett's dental rooms. No. 6, west side of public square, Winchester, Indiana.

8-1-1863

What Soldiers Receive

Any person enlisting in the armies of the United States will be entitled to the following after being mustered into the service: The sum of $100 bounty, of which $25 is paid upon being mustered, and $2 for recruiting pay, $13 per month, clothing and subsistence. The first month's pay is advanced to the recruit upon being mustered into service. Total payment in advance, $40. The remaining $75 bounty will be paid upon the expiration of the term of service, or in case of death, to the family of the soldier. In addition to the above, soldiers enlisting in Randolph County in the 69th get $50 bounty from the county.

5-21-1862

Advertisement: NEW GRAVE YARD!

The undersigned has laid off a New Grave Yard, immediately adjoining the old one, on the west, in lots 15 ½ by 19 ½ feet square, which he offers to sell on reasonable terms. Those desiring to secure a family burial place can now do so by calling early on DAVID HEASTON.

8-17-1865

The carpenter work of Mr. Klinck's fine residence, on the corner of Franklin and West streets, is now completed, and we think Mr. Klinck can certainly feel proud of it, for it certainly stands equal, if not above, any house in Winchester. Andrew J. Favorite was the principal workman, and is entitled to the patronage of the people of this place. We recommend all persons who are interested in good work to call and examine Mr. Klinck's house, as he will take pleasure in your calling for that purpose. And when you have a good job of work, Mr. Favorite will do it just right, if you will give him good lumber.

9-9-1864

Advertisement: LENKERSDORFER & WESP, Manufacturers of Furniture and Chairs, of the latest and best styles. East of Public Square, Winchester.

Advertisement: JOHN ROSS, Grocer and Baker, and dealer in Provisions. Store on the northeast corner of Main and Franklin Streets.

9-2-1858

WINCHESTER RETAIL MARKET

Flour per barrel	$5.50
Flaxseed per bushel	1.35
Corn Meal per bushel	50c
Wheat per bushel	85c
Barley per bushel	50c
Rye per bushel	50c
Corn per bushel	50c
Oats per bushel	50c
Potatoes per bushel	25c
Onions per bushel	40c
Turnips per bushel	20c
Lard per pound	9c

Butter per pound	10c
Cheese per pound	12c
Sugar per pound	12c
Coffee per pound	15c
Honey per pound	15c
Mackerel per pound	10c
Salt per barrel	$2.25
Tallow candles per pound	15c
White beans per bushel	$1.00
Hominy per pound	4c
Dayton crackers per pound	6c

3-1858

Randolph County Journal is published EVERY THURSDAY MORNING by Beverly & Smith. Our Terms:

> For twelve months in advance..............$1.50

> For six months in advance....................$1.00

All papers discontinued when the time subscribed for expires.

TERMS OF ADVERTISING:

> One square, 10 lines, one insertion............$1.00

> Each additional insertion....................... .25

> Quarter column one year.......................$25.00

Half..$35.00

One..$55.00

Legal advertisements must be paid for in advance

Unless a particular time is specified when handed in, advertisements will be published until ordered out, and charged accordingly.

4-3-1878

Announcements:

Dan Hoffman paid fifteen hundred dollars for his residence with six acres of ground attached to it just a few years ago. It would require about ten times that much to buy it now. He has one of the most beautiful places in town.

A postal card tacked up in the post office announces that the Young Men's Christian Association of New York will send male laborers, mechanics and such, to any part of the country who will work free of charge. True philanthropy.

There was a large congregation at the M.E. church last Sabbath to hear Rev. B.A. Kemp's farewell sermon. His sermon was a fine one and full of good advice. Four persons were received into full-membership and one baptized. His parting words to his congregation were touching and of such......(page cut off)

Geo. Ennis came very near entering the Kingdom of Heaven by way of a kerosene lamp last Saturday night.

Dave Fudge has sold the Jehiel Hull place, south of town, to Dave Wright, who will take possession immediately,

A geographical map of the United States, a pencil drawing, by W. A. Moorman, has been attracting general attention at the post office.

George Gerstner gave 'Squire Reed a handful of trade dollars and requested him to invest the same in chalk and slate pencils for the school children.

One Sinks, of Indianapolis, claims to the author of Luther Benson's "Fifteen Years in Hell". They have taken the matter to court. Benson has been drunk for the last two weeks.

We saw a man last Monday from the country, kick something on the sidewalk, which he supposed was a hat- he was doing as well as could be expected under the circumstances. Poor fellow, he "didn't know it was loaded."

6-1880

Old Settlers' Reunion

The next annual meeting of the Old Settlers of Randolph County will be held in the Fair Grounds at Winchester, on Saturday June 12th, 1880. The meeting should be remembered by all our people and a general attendance secured, the object being to unite for a day of general enjoyment and social talk over the customs, habits and doings of the early days of the men and women who settled up the country. These meetings should be encouraged and attended by all who feel an interest in preserving the reminiscences of our early history, as the parties who were there upon the scene of active life are fast passing away, and comparatively few are now remaining to tell of the thousands of interesting incidents that occurred within their knowledge; of the privations, hardships, social life and enjoyments incident to the settling up of a new country. Much has been done by this society in former years in gathering and preserving the sayings and doings of the pioneers, and much remains to be done before we shall have accomplished our work. Prof. Tucker is preparing a history of our county and hopes to have it sufficiently advanced to present on this occasion. The meeting will be called to order at 11 o'clock a.m. and miscellaneous exercises will happen for one hour, when there will be an adjournment of one hour for the regular picnic dinner, after which the exercises will consist of speeches, music and songs. An effort will be made to procure the services of distinguished pioneers for the occasion.

Asahel Stone, President

4-3-1872

Article   (If this doesn't make you smile, nothing will!)

The usual quiet of Meridian Street was disturbed yesterday afternoon by a collision between two well-known ladies of this place. The attacking party used eggs as her weapon, and was supported by her daughter, armed with woman's usual weapon of warfare-a broom. The lady thus attacked was taken by surprise but after being pretty well peppered with eggs, went for her assailants, when they beat a hasty retreat. She followed them closely, and clinched her principal antagonist, and hair and "sich" flew for a few minutes, the daughter in the meantime keeping up a bombardment with the broom. At the conclusion of the encounter, the parties repaired to Squire Reed's office, where the attacking party paid $20 fine and $2 costs for her little diversion. A suit for damages is now threatened, and the case is not ended yet. We give no names, because our readers in town know who the parties are, and it would do no good to publish them to strangers.

8-17-1865

A young lady who entered upon the solemn duties of a wife, within the last month, in a pleasant village in this State, has served a notice on the liquor dealers of the place to not sell her husband any more liquor, or she will commence a prosecution against the violating parties. We think she has a bright future before her.

5-1858

Advertisements

NEBBARD'S New Drug Store, No. 5 Commercial Row, Winchester, Indiana, keeps Drugs, Patent Medicines, toilet soaps, perfumery paper and envelopes, toys, fancy articles, lamps, lanterns, paints, oils, varnishes, and dye. Stuff's constantly on hand.

EDGER, KIZER & Co. Butter and Eggs, Feathers, Beeswax, Wheat, Corn, &c. THE HIGHEST MARKET PRICES PAID Farmers, bring along your produce. Warerooms opposite the Bellefontaine Passenger Depot, Winchester.

4-1873

An ad appeared for the Bee Line Railroad with a schedule for passenger trains leaving and arriving in Winchester. Destinations included the following stations: Union, Bellfountaine, Crestline, Cleveland, Buffalo, Niagara Falls, Rochester, Albany, Boston and New York City.

They also advertised sleeping cars.

6-3-1885

"Last Saturday was Memorial Day, and the interest manifested by all classes of our citizens was more general that usual. During the day many of the business houses and private residences were tastily and handsomely decorated with the flag of the Union. Business houses were closed and business generally suspended from 1 to 4 o'clock p.m., while the interest of all centered in the silent cities of the dead, where sleep so many brave and gallant heroes who gave up their lives that the free institutions of our country should be forever perpetuated.

The procession was formed promptly at 1 0'clock by J.K. Martin, Marshall of the Day, in the order named in the programme, and marched to the old cemetery, where the procession halted, while the Committee detailed b the Post for that purpose, decorated the graves of the following named comrades: David Heaston, John Way and Jehiel Hull, War of 1812; James Rady, Xerxes Jones, Henry Voris, Michael Voris, Erastus Reed, William Magee, A.O. Neff, Abram and S. Heaston, Jesse May, O.P Boyden, James H. Bowen Samuel McClure, W.L Steele, Augustus Steele, Henry Way, Martin R. Thomas, Lafayette Deardoff and Dr. Frazier. When these decorations were completed the procession marched to Fountain Park Cemetery, where the graves of Ezra Stone, war of 1812, J. Lawrence Neff, John Enos Neff, William Alexander, William Pohlman, John Heaston, Alfred Hogston Clint D. Smith and James E. Williamson were decorated. After the graves had been decorated, the people assembled on the Soldiers' lot, where the Post Commander delivered a short address, after which there was a prayer by the chaplain, songs by the choir, a dirge by the band, and the cenotaph was decorated by the Sunday School children. Gen. Shanks, the orator of the day, was introduced and had just begun his speech when a rain storm came up and everything came to a sudden ending. It was and is a matter of general regret that the speech could not be delivered, and the General had started out in a manner that indicated he had a well prepared and interesting speech for the occasion."

I end this chapter with the last article. It is important because it lists many of the soldiers still in the Old Winchester as late as 1885. The remains of some soldiers were moved after that date and are now in Fountain Park. There are some errors of omission (see list of soldiers buried in the Old Winchester) and I have Jehiel Hall in the Civil War, not the War of 1812, but it is gratifying to learn about the patriotism of the citizenry at that time.

A Last Few Words from the Author

I am a registered nurse, not a writer. Luckily for me much of the information in this book came directly from sources that could be quoted, so my "creativity" was not significantly challenged, which is a good thing. There were two periods of time when I was intensely involved in putting the book together. The first was when I was researching for information about the people buried in the graveyard. That involved many months of going through old files and microfilm and living on the computer, especially ancestry.com. The second was when I was actually putting everything together in some logical order and then typing it.

During those periods I was often preoccupied. Someone may have said to me "How are the grandchildren?" and I might have responded "In 1849 Winchester had a population of 750 people." A simple inquiry into how the book was coming along might result in a reply something like this: "Did you know that almost all their bread was made from corn?" What I am trying to say is that it takes a lot of focus to write a book, even if it is mostly historical and reference material. And it can make you a little crazy!

People would often make comments like "Life was simple back then wasn't it?" Let's see, use an ax to cut down trees, use the trees to build a cabin, put a chimney and fireplace in the cabin to heat it and to cook the food, chop down more trees to make space for growing corn, plant the corn, harvest the corn, ride your horse to Cincinnati with a bag of corn to have it ground, return home, make the corn bread over the fire in the fireplace, eat and enjoy....... or order a pizza for delivery. Hmm.....

The circumstances of our lives, then and now, are so different. But if I could recapture anything from the people in this book, it would be their value system, their industriousness, their willingness to help each other, their strong belief in hard work and self-reliance, their moral code and their belief in religious freedom. Add to that their absolute belief that their right to life, liberty and the pursuit of happiness was all they really needed to come to the Wild West and create their dreams and succeed. And they did.

Bibliography

Ancestry.com., on-line fee-based databases, U.S. Census Records, Family Histories, Military Data, www.ancestry.com.

Branson, Ronald, Indiana Pioneer Life, www.countyhistory.com, 2000-2006.

Burial Records, Fountain Park Cemetery, Winchester, Indiana, pre-1880 deaths.

Carmack, Sharon DeBartolo, Your Guide to Cemetery Research, Betterway Books, Cincinnati, Ohio, 2002.

Connecticut Gravestone Network, Reading Gravestone Inscriptions, www.ctgravestones.com.

Department of Health and Human Services, National Center for Health Statistics, 2006.

Farmland Enterprise, Reunion of Diggs, Way and Moorman Families, Farmland, Indiana, June 17, 1904.

Harrell-Sesniak, Mary, Genealogy Blog, Understanding Terms Found in Historical Newspapers, blog.genealogybank.com, Feb.11, 1013

Headstones, Wikipedia, www.wikipedia.org/wiki/gravestones.

Indiana Historical Society, Indiana Newspapers on Microfilm, U.S. National Endowment for the Humanities, 1980-2006 project dates.

Meyer, Richard E., Cemeteries and Gravemarkers, Voices of American Culture, Utah State University Press, Logan, Utah, 1992.

Old Medical Terms, Fention Historical Society, Fenton, Michigan, http://fentonhistsoc.tripod.com, 2012.

Randolph County, Indiana, Portrait and Biographical Record, A.W. Bowen and Co., Chicago, 1894.

Spindel, Connie, Graveyard Inscriptions Explained, www.freepages. genealogy.rootsweb.ancestry.com, March 20, 2001.

Starbuck, Dane, The Goodriches: An American Family, Liberty Fund, 2001.

Strangstad, Lynette, A Graveyard Preservation Primer, Alta Mira Press, Walnut Creek, CA,1995.

Tucker, Ebenezer, History of Randolph County Indiana, A.L. Klingman, Chicago, 1882.